INSIGHT POCKET GUIDE

DenmaRK

DISCOVERY CHANNEL

APA PUBLICATIONS

Part of the Langenscheidt Publishing Group

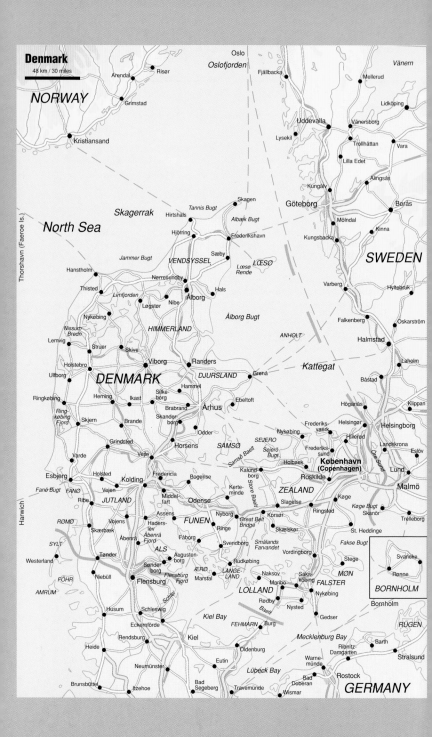

Denmark

48 km / 30 miles

NORWAY

North Sea

Skagerrak

SWEDEN

DENMARK

Kattegat

JUTLAND

FUNEN

ZEALAND

København (Copenhagen)

BORNHOLM

LOLLAND

FALSTER

MØN

GERMANY

Welcome!

This guidebook combines the interests and enthusiasms of two of the world's best-known information providers: Insight Guides, who have set the standard for visual travel guides since 1970, and Discovery Channel, the world's premier source of non-fiction television programming. It brings you the best of Denmark in tailor-made itineraries devised by Insight's correspondent, Jo Hermann.

Denmark's pleasures are low-key but satisfying, qualities summed up by the Danish word *hygge,* which is used to convey a feeling of being at ease – relaxing at a summer concert, for example, having drinks with friends or curling up with a good book. Exploring the country's white beaches, attractive villages, medieval castles and Viking ruins, the tours are based on three key areas: Copenhagen and Surroundings, Århus and Around, and North Jutland. Each section has its own full-day and half-day tours and excursions, into which are crammed a whole range of sights and activities. Supporting the itineraries are sections on history and culture, shopping, eating out, nightlife and festivals, plus a detailed practical information section.

Jo Hermann has been working as a writer and editor for the past 15 years – including three years spent in Houston, Texas as a TV journalist. She was born and brought up in Denmark, yet, she says, until she was 15 had never even visited a Danish castle or manor house. Her eyes were opened to her country's wealth of history and landscape when she began to study architecture. Since then she has travelled the length and breadth of Denmark. In this guide she shares some of her discoveries with you.

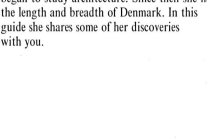

C O N T E N T S

*Pages 2/3:
Superb cycling
country*

Experimentarium

Pages 8/9: Opera fans in Copenhagen

HISTORY

Denmark has changed drastically in size through the years. Its present border was established as late as 1920, when the people of Slesvig voted to live on the Danish side of the border. The result of this vote was that Northern Slesvig 'came home' to Denmark, while the southern part of the old duchy united with Germany. This partitioning was the culmination of 1700 years of strife, war and migration during which the Danes had alternately attempted to control other countries and struggled to survive as a nation. I will try to make a long story short.

Grave Mounds are still visible

The Beginning

The first people to set foot in Jutland some 240,000 years ago were pre-Neanderthals who were hunting reindeer. But the ice forced them away again. The first hunters who stayed didn't arrive until around 12,000BC. Deep dark woods covered the country then, but around 4200BC something happened: a new group of people moved in, the first farmers. They began to burn the trees and cultivate the land and in the ground they found flint, a prime material for axes and sharp tools. The farmers buried their dead in grave mounds, some of which are still visible in today's landscape.

Around 1800BC traders from the south introduced bronze, and new wealth reached the country. The metal came from southeast Europe and was traded for amber, cattle and fur. Around 500BC, when iron replaced bronze, the picture changed again. Iron was harder and could be produced locally, and made it possible for the farmers to develop new tools and more efficient techniques. Cultivated land slowly began to replace the woods. The country was becoming more populous, and people began to fight each other for land. Around 250BC a number of tribes from North Jutland began to migrate towards the south.

The next wave of migration came north. Around 200AD, the Danes left North Germany to settle in Scania (South Sweden) and on Zealand, where they drove out the original population. Some 300 years later, they had taken Jutland as well and *Danmark* had come into being.

Viking Ship

The Vikings

In the second half of the 8th century, the Scandinavians designed a new kind of boat: a long, slim and slightly arched vessel that could come ashore at just about any type of coast. And it did. The Vikings soon became feared from Italy to Greenland and from Ireland to Russia. The different nations all participated in the pillaging: in general, the Norwegian Vikings stayed in the north, while the Swedes went east, and the Danes took care of England and Western Europe.

The Viking Age is often counted from 793, when the monks at Lindisfarne in Northumberland were the very first to

receive uninvited guests from the north. Until then, people had considered it impossible to travel any distance on the high seas; but the Vikings could go much further than this.

In 806 the Danes attacked Ireland; in 810 the Frisians received a visit; in 843 Danish Vikings sailed up the river Loire to Nantes, and the following year they scared the Moors in Spain; in 845 Paris paid a ransom in order not to be attacked, but another group of Vikings hit them later; and around 900 Normandy became a Danish Viking colony. The Danes ruled in north-east England from 871, and they kept fighting until king Canute (Knud in Danish) had gained power over the entire country in 1016. They were forced back in 1066, when William the Conqueror won the Battle of Hastings and occupied England. Another Danish prince Knud returned to try to regain England a decade later, but without success. After three centuries, the Viking Age was finally over, and Denmark began to shrink again.

The Vikings didn't listen to prayers, didn't feel obliged to keep their promises, didn't shy away from sly tricks and even attacked other Viking countries. Still, they were not quite as barbaric as legend has it. Some historians even maintain that they were welcomed by the British women, because they washed themselves on a regular basis. But the best evidence of their level of cultural achievement was in their villages. We know four of them, all extremely well-organised: Trelleborg on West Zealand, Nonnebakken on Funen, Fyrkat in Hobro in central Jutland, and Aggersborg close to Limfjorden in North Jutland. The houses are laid out along straight lines, either radiating from the centre or in square blocks across two axes, with a circular rampart to protect each village. These villages show that the Vikings must have been skilled in geometry – the same knowledge that enabled them to travel all over Europe without losing their way.

Building in Stone

In the 12th century the Danes learned to build in stone and tile. Although this new technique was too expensive to apply to ordinary houses, it was not so for God's house. In the 12th century alone, 2,000 communities erected stone churches, most of which are still standing. They were built in either the heavy Romanesque style or the more elegant Gothic style and richly decorated with frescoes. Church towers were not yet in fashion at the time of building, but were added later. At the time of the Reformation, the churches were whitewashed to erase all traces of their Catholic past, but many of the frescoes have since been recovered.

The aristocracy also built their houses in stone. Since farming was the main source of income for both rich and poor, most of the manor houses were built in the country. They reflect the style of their time (and the wallet of the builder) and range from large farm houses to castles with towers and moats, to elegant palaces. The churches and manor houses are a real architectural treasure, unique to Denmark.

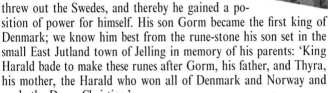

Church fresco detail

A Christian Nation

Gorm den Gamle (Gorm the Old) was the first king to rule over the country called Denmark, and the members of the royal family descend from this old man.

Before the 900s, the country had been inhabited by tribes who regarded themselves as neighbours and kinsmen, but felt no need to organise themselves under one ruler. Matters were settled locally, but attacks from Swedish Vikings and general unrest in the early 900s paved the road for a strong man to take command. Hardeknud was the one who threw out the Swedes, and thereby he gained a position of power for himself. His son Gorm became the first king of Denmark; we know him best from the rune-stone his son set in the small East Jutland town of Jelling in memory of his parents: 'King Harald bade to make these runes after Gorm, his father, and Thyra, his mother, the Harald who won all of Denmark and Norway and made the Danes Christian.'

During the next three centuries Denmark was constantly engaged in war, even after the Viking Age had ended. Germany was the main target, because the Germans controlled most of the trade in the Baltic region. In 1397, Denmark, Norway and Sweden finally teamed up to drive out the Germans, who had occupied a good part of Jutland and Sweden, Stockholm included. The union was spearheaded by Queen Margrethe I, who eventually became the ruler of all three countries. But the notion of brotherhood between the Scandinavians never really caught on; the Swedes pulled out, and years of exhausting wars with Germany and Sweden followed.

Meanwhile, the revolutionary theses of Martin Luther had reached Copenhagen. In 1536, King Christian III jumped on this chance to wrestle power and possessions from the hands of the Catholic church – realising that this was really the only way to pay the huge national debt the wars had incurred. Thus it was that Denmark became a Lutheran country.

Around the end of the 16th century, Christian IV entered the scene as the most enterprising king Denmark has ever had. He had a keen interest in architecture, music, shipbuilding, trade, farming, warfare, you name it. He wouldn't leave it to his secretary to write his letters, and he wouldn't leave it to the archi-

King Christian III

Christian IV's Rosenborg Castle

tects to design his buildings. He was directly responsible for the design of the Round Tower, Rosenborg Castle and many others in Copenhagen. Unfortunately, he was just as convinced about his abilities as a general, and he engaged in new wars with Sweden that continued long after his death. The country was once again in debt, and as the aristocracy refused to pay its share, so the heaviest burden fell on the merchants. They responded by supporting the monarchy against the aristocracy. At a quiet revolution in 1660, King Frederik III was given absolute power.

During the reign of the enterprising Christian IV, Denmark had founded its first colony Trankebar in Ceylon, and the colonial trade grew rapidly. Throughout the 18th century, Danish merchants made huge profits from such trade. Wars between the English and the French had the effect of cutting France off from its colonies, and Denmark jumped at the chance to sell its own colonial produce to France. The British were not amused, and in 1801 they sent Lord Nelson to Copenhagen, where he defeated a haphazardly gathered fleet of floats and worn-out battle ships. Six years later, when Denmark had sided with Napoleon, the British returned and bombed the city back into poverty. The fire lasted three days and when it was over, the British navy sailed away with what was left of the fleet.

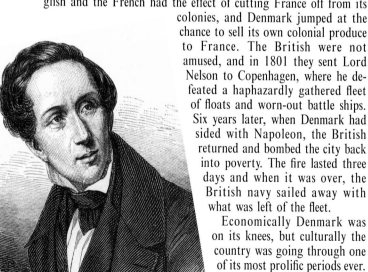

Economically Denmark was on its knees, but culturally the country was going through one of its most prolific periods ever.

Hans Christian Andersen

Hans Christian Andersen wrote his fairy tales and novels, while Søren Kierkegaard pondered the essential questions of being, and in Rome a host of painters and sculptors gathered around Bertel Thorvaldsen, who sold his classical marble statues all over Europe. August Bournonville studied in Paris, but returned to Copenhagen to introduce his new techniques at the Royal Ballet. Hans Christian Ørsted discovered the electro-magnetic field, and Rasmus Rask found the first traces of the Indo-European language. It was a golden age at a low budget.

The Coming of Democracy

Inspired by the French revolutions, Danish liberals demanded a new constitution in 1848. Since the government wouldn't listen, the citizens went straight to the king, who would. It took another year to work out the specifics of the constitution and 50 years of feuds between the two chambers, the Rigsdagen and the Folketinget, to implement it. The aristocracy of the Rigsdagen simply issued provisionary emergency laws so that it could have its own way. But while the aristocracy ruled, the people proved that they were quite capable of handling their own affairs. The farmers organised dairy co-ops, where one man had one vote, no matter if he had 10 or 30 cows. They also sought to improve their skills at the folk high schools that the visionary priest Grundtvig had started for people of little or no education.

The farmers had their co-operatives and the workers their unions. Meanwhile in the cities, the Social Democratic Party had been growing, and in 1924 it was their turn to form a government. Tobacco worker Thorvald Stauning became prime minister and stayed in power with only one interruption until his death in 1942. During this period, the country went a long way down the road towards social democracy. Since 1933, begging has become a thing of the past – Denmark believes the needy have a *right* to be helped.

Germans advance on Denmark in 1940

When the Germans invaded Denmark on their way to Norway in 1940, Stauning decided not to fight. He thought that Denmark should be under German 'protection' until the war was over, and that meanwhile it could remain an independent nation. But some people didn't agree. The resistance movement kept growing, and after a general strike in 1943, the government resigned and the Germans took over. Later the same year, the Germans decided to deport the Danish Jews, but they only managed to round up 500 people; members of the resistance movement had helped another 6,500 across the sound to Sweden.

Denmark had fully recovered from the war by the beginning of the 1960s and began to experience tremendous economic growth. The Social Democrats had set the agenda: the new wealth should reach everybody. A comprehensive welfare system was set up, funded by relatively high taxation levels, raising the standard of living for ordinary people to one of the highest in the world. But the money was, to a large extent, borrowed and the world-wide oil crisis in 1973 hit hard. By 1982 a right-wing coalition, led by Conservative Poul Schlüter brought inflation under control and reduced Danish foregn debt – helped by the country becoming nearly self-sufficient in energy as a result of North Sea oil and natural gas discoveries. In 1993, a Social Democratic coalition came to power, led by Poul Nyrup Rasmussen. It has focused on maintaining and reforming the welfare state and helping to move Denmark to a position of advantage in an era of increased international competition and European integration.

Margrethe II, Queen of Denmark since 1972

However, it is a burdened Denmark that moves into the 21st century, with welfare, health and education buckling under the strain of government austerity as the national debt continues to grow. Meanwhile, the country's relaxed pace of life has been speeded up in recent years. By 2000, every other Dane owned a mobile cell phone. In addition, a system of bridges has replaced ferries, making transport fast and efficient. The most recent, the Øresund Fixed Link from Copenhagen to Mamö, Sweden, has formed the eighth largest urban region in Europe, attracting several international companies to the area.

Denmark has been a member of the EU since 1972, but has kept itself in the spotlight by turning down key resolutions: the Maastricht treaty in 1992 (though a modified Amsterdam treaty was approved in 1993) and in 2000, the common Euro currency.

Historical Highlights

12000BC The first hunters arrive.

4200–1800 The Stone Age. Tools are made of flint and ceramics.

1800–500 The Bronze Age. Trade with the rest of Europe.

500BC–AD1000 The Iron Age. Farming develops.

300 First traces of battles between tribes on Danish ground.

AD200 The Danes settle on the islands and later in Jutland.

800–1050 The Viking Age. Vikings plunder Europe.

960 King Harald Bluetooth is christened. During his reign Denmark becomes one nation.

12th century About 2,000 stone churches are built.

1200 A new market for herring in Scania attracts traders far and wide.

1219 King Valdemar II conquers Estonia. For a short while, he controls the whole coastline from South Jutland to Estonia.

1397 Denmark unites with Norway and Sweden in the Kalmar Union, ruled by Margrethe I.

1536 The Reformation. Denmark becomes a Lutheran country.

1596–1648 Christian IV rules.

1640–1720 80 years of wars with Sweden.

1660 Absolute monarchy is introduced with Frederik III.

1728 & 1795 Fires ravage Copenhagen.

1733–88 Due to shortage of labourers in the country, farmers are denied the right to move away from their home districts.

1801 The British admiral Nelson defeats the Danes in a naval battle at Copenhagen, caused by a conflict of interest in the colonial trade.

1807 England forces Denmark out of its neutrality in the Napoleonic wars, then bombs Copenhagen and destroys the Danish fleet.

1813 Denmark declares national bankruptcy.

1814 Denmark's allegiance to Napoleon means that the country suffers reparations after Napoleon's defeat – and loses Norway.

1830 Recovering from the war, the people demand a voice in the administration of the country.

1835 The first fairy tales by Hans Christian Andersen are published.

1848 Christian VII dies. 15,000 citizens march to the new king Frederik VII to demand a constitution. When they arrive the government has already resigned.

1864 In a bloody battle, Denmark loses Slesvig-Holstein to Germany.

1866–1901 The aristocracy rule, assisted by emergency laws.

1901 The aristocracy resigns, and the constitution is finally effective.

1915 Women and servants achieve the right to vote.

1920 Parts of Slesvig are won back in a peaceful settlement.

1920 King Christian X dissolves the government, but is reproved by his people.

1924 The Social Democrats form their first government.

1933 Social reforms guarantee all citizens the right to unemployment benefits and state-funded pensions.

1940–45 German occupation.

1949 Denmark joins NATO.

1953 Princess Margrethe becomes heir to the throne, due to a revision of the constitution; the Rigsdagen is abolished.

1972 Denmark joins the EC.

1992 Danes refuse to ratify the Maastricht treaty, passing a revised Amsterdam Treaty in 1993.

1998 The Great Belt Bridge is completed, connecting Zealand by road to Funen and the mainland for the first time.

2000 The Danes refuse to join the Euro currency. The Øresund Fixed Link opens, joining Copenhagen to Malmö, Sweden.

Copenhagen - City Centre

200 m / 220 yards

- - - - Itinerary 1
- - - - Itinerary 2

SØLVGADE

Fredericiagade

Fischers Gade

Borgergade

Adelgade

ROSENBORG HAVE

Kronprinsessegade

Dronningens

KONGENS HAVE
(KING'S GARDEN)

Adelgade

Borgergade

Store Kongensgade

Fredericiagade

Marmorkirken
(Marble Church)

Frederiksgade

Amaliegade

Amalienborg
Palace

Amalienborg
Plads

AMALIEHAVEN

Tværgade

Bredgade

Palægade

Amaliegade

Larsens Plads

Kvæsthusbroen

Dokøen

Nyhavnsgade

Menstergade

Ny Østergad

Gothersgade

Ny Adelgade

Grønn.
Pistolstr.
Gl. Mønt

Sværtegade

Østergade

Kongens Nytorv

Hotel
d'Angleterre

Charlottenborg

Nyhavn

Sankt Annæ Plads

Toldbodgade

Kvæsthusgade

H.C.
Andersen's
House

museum

Royal Theatre

Vingårdstræde

Nyhavn

Herluf Trolles

gertory

Fortunstr.

Bremerholm

Peder Skrams

Holbergsgade

rvaldsens
Museum

Højbro
Pladsen

Admiralsg.

Ved Stranden

Niels Juels G.

Tordenskjoldsg.

Holmenskanal

Holmens Church

Havnegade

Inderhavnen

Kroyers-
plads

Bodenhofs Plads

SLOTSHOLMEN

Christiansborg
Slotsplads

Havnegade

Gammel
Dok

Wilders Plads

Burmestersg.

iansborg

Christians Kanal

Børsgade

Slotsholmsgade

Knippels bro

Start

Strandgade

Overgaden neden Vandet

Wilders Plads

Bådsmandsstræde

Prinsessegade

Naval
Museum

Christiania

National
Library

Christians Brygge

Christian's
Church

Wildersgade

Overgaden oven Vandet

Sankt Annæ Gade

Christianshavns
Torv market

Our Saviour's
Church

Løvens
Bastion

Langebrogade

Christianshavns Voldgade

Dronningensgade

Prinsessegade

Torvegade

Langebro

Kalvebod
Bastion

Enhjørningens
Bastion

Panterens
Bastion

Elefantens
Bastion

Christmas
Møllers
Plads

Copenhagen & Surroundings

DAY 1

From Havn to København

The heart of Copenhagen: a day-long route that takes in Strøget, Nyhavn, Amalienborg Palace, Rosenborg Castle, Rundetårn, Helligåndskirken, the National Museum, Larsbjørnsstræde, Gråbrødre Torv, with shopping, coffee and lunch along the way. Evening at Café Sommersko.

– *Starting point: Rådhuspladsen (The Town Hall Square), close to the central train station and on the route of most city buses. Buy a money-saving Copenhagen Card (CC) at the tourist information office near Tivoli and the train station. The changing of the guards*

at Amalienborg Palace takes place at noon; if you start around 9am, you should have plenty of time to get there. –

In 1962 Copenhagen closed its central shopping street to traffic and turned it into a pedestrian street 1.6km (1 mile) long. All kinds of people have taken **Strøget** to heart. Shoppers, street vendors, musicians, jugglers, chess players and tourists rub elbows with political crusaders and busy office workers, so the street is often crowded and rarely boring. But if you get up early, you'll soon discover that most people don't. The majority of the shops don't

Left: Strøget juggler

Copenhagen and Christiansborg Palace

open until 10am, and you'll have the opportunity to see the city come slowly alive.

From Rådhuspladsen, the first 250m (270yds) of Strøget covers the area where the original Viking hamlet of Havn was situated. The place was also known as Købmændenes Havn (The Merchants' Harbour) or, in short, København – the name still in use. Protected by the island of Amager, Havn provided a safe hiding place where pirates could be kept at a distance.

In 1167, King Valdemar gave Havn to his foster brother Absalon, who was the bishop of Roskilde, and he built his castle on an islet between Havn and Amager. He also extended the size of the hamlet considerably by building a rampart around the area from Rådhuspladsen to Kongens Nytorv (the full length of Strøget) and from his castle to Nørreport. This area is also known as the medieval city, and even today, it is still the heart of Copenhagen. The city has had a long history of wars and fires, and consequently very few buildings are left from that period, but the layout of the streets has remained almost the same as in those early days.

On Strøget

The first open space you'll come to is actually two squares: **Gammeltorv** and **Nytorv** (Old and New Square). Until the last big fire in 1795, they were separated by a town hall, but today they appear as one. In the centre of Gammeltorv stands the **Karitasbrønden** (Well of Charity), which was built in 1608. It was given to the people as a public well by the avid builder-king Christian IV. The well has been dramatically altered by later generations, who elevated the original figures, added a new foundation and called it a fountain. This is a popular meeting place.

The Stork Fountain

Walk on down Strøget to **Amagertorv** with Storkespringvandet (the Stork Fountain) and some of the best and most expensive shops in Copenhagen (we'll get back to that). If you look to the right, you'll see Christiansborg (the Parliament building) behind Højbro Square. Turn left two blocks further down Strøget into the passage named **Pistolstræde** (yes, Pistol Street, so called because of its shape). A century ago, this was the worst slum area in the city, but nowadays it is downright chic. If you skipped breakfast this morning, you can make up for it at the bakery **Konditoriet** here.

When you get to the square where the pistol handle starts, there's a passage leading out into **Grønnegade**. Here you'll find a modern shop selling copies of jewellery made during the Bronze, Iron and Viking Ages. When you've taken a look at that continue across Ny Østergade. The first street to your right will be Ny Adelgade, where Tage Andersen has his trend-setting flower shop at number 12. His dramatic creations made with fresh and dried flowers and branches in metal containers have added new life to many a dull windowsill.

Ny Adelgade leads up to **Kongens Nytorv** (the King's New Square). The king in question was Frederik III, successor to Christian IV. Frederik ordered several new squares to be built as part of a grander scheme to modernise Copenhagen, among them Kongens Nytorv. If you walk to the right, you'll find the grand Hotel d'Angleterre, Denmark's top hotel, in the first of the mansions. Further up to the right is the department store Magasin du Nord, and across the street lies **The Royal Theatre** (Det Kongelige Teater; tours Sundays 11am; adults 75kr, children 35kr), a neo-renaissance building dating from 1874. Continue to the brown brick mansion of **Charlottenborg**, home of the Royal Academy of Fine Arts (Monday–Friday 10am–5pm). To reach the exhibition building in the back you must walk through

Guarding Amalienborg Palace

the two courtyards. In the hallway are bulletin boards with posters from art galleries all around the city and country, so this is the place for a quick overview of the best of what the current shows have to offer.

When you leave, take the exit to the right, and you'll be standing on the bank of **Nyhavn Canal** (New Harbour). It used to be that Nyhavn had a nice and a naughty side. You are standing on the nice side. A few tattoo shops across the water still tell the story of what Nyhavn once was, but today, it is simply a charming restaurant strip and a nice place to stop, whether you are ready for lunch or just for a cup of coffee.

Amalienborg Palace

During the summer, tour boats leave from Nyhavn for cruises of the harbour area – typically the route will take in Slotsholmen, Christianshavn and the Little Mermaid. This is one of the least expensive and most memorable sightseeing tours in the city, and is particularly recommended if the weather is fine. Children travel half price on these tours.

Back on land again, walk along the restaurant side of Nyhavn and follow the waterfront around the corner and past the Oslo boat until you come to the **Amaliehaven** park. The Queen of Denmark resides at the **Amalienborg Palace** behind the fountain. At noon, fresh guardsmen come in to replace their tired colleagues. How many soldiers you'll get to see in this changing of the guards depends on how many members of the royal family are in town. If the flag is flying, the Queen is home. In the summer, when the royals have taken off for their country residences, the show is somewhat less spectacular, but the place is still impressive. The statue in the centre of the square depicts Frederik V, who designed the palace in 1749. It is one of the finest equestrian statues in the world, and small wonder – it took the French sculptor Saly 20 years to finish it. The **Amalienborg Collection** (11am–4pm, closed Mondays in winter, adults 35kr, children 5kr) occupies a wing of the palace and features exhibits from 19th and 20th century Danish royal collections.

Behind the palace lies **Marmorkirken** (the Marble Church), easily recognisable by its huge cupola. The statues around it portray some of the greatest Danish names in religious philosophy, among them Søren Kierkegaard and N.F.S. Grundtvig, who founded the folk high schools *(see the History section)* and wrote the words for many of the hymns in the Danish song book. Store Kongensgade

Nyhavn Canal for cafes and restaurants

runs behind the church. Make a left turn along it and walk back towards Kongens Nytorv. Shortly before you get to the square, look for the **Bolten's** sign to the right. If you need to rest your legs, there are plenty of options in this little complex of cafes and bars; a good place for lunch. At the back end of Bolten's, you'll come out onto Gothersgade.

Turn right and follow the street to the first traffic lights. In front of you **Kongens Have** (the King's Garden) opens up, also known as Rosenborg Have after its castle. Follow the path to the fountain and continue to the other end of the park. To get to **Rosenborg Castle**, you'll have to exit the park, turn onto Øster Voldgade and find the entrance from the street (July–September: 10am–5pm; May–June: 10am–4pm; November–April: 11am–2pm, closed Monday; adults 50kr, children 10kr). There's no electric light in the castle.

Rosenborg was one of Christian IV's many projects, and he designed a good part of it himself. It was originally planned as the summer residence of the royal family, just outside the city, and three generations of kings have spent time there. But as the city grew, the royal family decided to move their 'summerhouse' out to Frederiksberg.

Rosenborg has been a museum since 1838, and it was one of the first of its kind to be arranged chronologically. The first three rooms you'll see were used by Christian IV, the next one by his successor Frederik III and so forth. The last king to be represented is Frederik VII, who in 1849 signed Denmark's first democratic constitution, then happily declared that from now on, he'd sleep late in the morning. In room 3, you'll find a true rarity: the clothes Christian IV was wearing during a battle with the Germans in which his eye was pierced. The bloodstains are still visible on the collar and the handkerchief. But apart from this curious

The Marble Church

piece, Rosenborg also has marvellous treasures of ornate furniture, paintings and tableware accumulated by the monarchy from the 16th to 19th century and the royal crown jewels.

When you leave the castle, turn left along Øster Voldgade and then left again at pedestrianised Frederiksborggade, which leads into Købmagergade. Along here on the left is another of Christian IV's buildings, **Rundetårn** (the Round Tower; summer: Monday–Saturday 10am–8pm, Sunday noon–8pm; winter: Monday–Saturday 10am–5pm, Sunday noon–5pm; adults 15kr, children 5kr).

The tower was built originally as an observatory, and amateur astronomers still use it today for observations on clear winter nights. From the top, you'll also have a splendid view over the rooftops of Copenhagen. The many towers and spires serve as landmarks in an otherwise flat city, and if you can memorise just a few of them, you'll never lose your way. The spiral walkway to the top of Rundetårn is unique in European architecture; children love to hide in the many niches and to race down the walkway. Halfway up, the old library above Trinitatis Church has been turned into a gallery with changing exhibitions of arts and crafts.

Down again, turn left and walk back to Strøget for a bit of window-shopping. On Amagertorv you'll find three of the most exquisite shops in Copenhagen gathered within one block. Start with the silverware in **Georg Jensen**, then work your way through

Working in Kongens Have

Rundetårn's spiral walkway

the **Royal Copenhagen Porcelain** shop to **Illums Bolighus** to look at modern design (I recommend you read the chapter on shopping in this book before you start buying). The stores are all owned by the united breweries of Tuborg and Carlsberg, who have always had a strong interest in the arts.

If you follow Strøget back the way you came this morning, you'll soon come to **Helligåndskirken** (Church of the Holy Ghost). The church interior dates from the late 19th century, but the adjacent building to the left goes all the way back to the 15th century, when it was built by a religious order to function as a hospital for the poor.

Look for the passage called Klostergården across from the church. The peace and silence in this 1920s archway is a striking contrast to the noise of Strøget. It leads to Læderstræde, where the better end of Copenhagen's antique and carpet shops are located. Follow Nabeløstræde down to Gammel Strand, and you'll be standing on the old shore-line facing Slotsholmen, where Absalon built his (long-gone) castle. The narrow street to your right, **Snaregade**, is one of the oldest in the city. Several of the houses are from the 16th century and survived the fire of 1728. If you can get into No 4 (ask a resident), you'll see all the owners of the houses on this particular lot from 1397 to 1912 depicted on the walls.

When you reach Rådhusstræde, turn left, follow Frederiksholms Kanal and turn right at Ny Vestergade. Half way down the street stands the **National Museum** (Nationalmuseet; daily 10am–5pm, closed Monday; adults 40 kr, free on Wednesdays, children free). Built as a palace in the 1740's, this is the largest museum in the country. Buy your ticket, head back towards the entrance and make a left turn. That will take you to the old Danish collection. To get the chronology right, walk all the way down through the glass-covered walkway to the rune-stone hall and turn right. All

signs are written in both English and Danish, and you can easily spend an hour studying the collections. However, if you want only the highlights and haven't got much time, you should disregard the chronology, turn left from the room with the *lur* trumpets and just go through the Bronze Age and Viking collections. The rune-stone hall will then signal the end of the trip. But don't forget to take a look at the eerie room next to the *lurs*, where four people lie in their hollow oak coffins, the way they were buried in a peat bog ages ago.

Head back the way you came along Rådhusstræde across Gammeltorv. The third street on your left will be Skt. Peders Stræde with **Skt. Petri Kirke** on the corner. Although partly rebuilt, this is the oldest church in central Copenhagen with a chapel that dates back to the 13th century. The church belongs to the German congregation, and unfortunately you can only see it from the outside. Turn left, and you'll enter the bohemian neighbourhood of **Larsbjørnstræde**, usually at its most active in the late afternoon, which is about the time you should be there if you've followed this itinerary. This is the place to buy second-hand clothes, organic vegetables, Indian jewellery, old comic books and the like, or just to hang out and watch people go by.

When you have tired of that, follow Vestergade back towards Gammeltorv and continue almost to the end of the street, where **Gråbrødretorv** lies to your right. The Franciscan monks (the Greyfriars who gave the square its name) built their monastery here in the 13th century, but times have changed. Today, it is more like Nyhavn without the water. For your evening's leisure you can pick and choose among the restaurants and bars (**Peder Oxe** is always a safe bet), or if the weather's fine just enjoy a cool bottle of beer in the shade of the old plane tree.

Royal ironwork

If you find prices too stiff (or if you'd like a cup of coffee after dinner), walk across the square to Løvstræde, turn right at Købmagergade and left at the second street, Kronprinsensgade, home of **Café Sommersko**. Sommersko was the first real cafe in Denmark, and it is still among the liveliest at night. I like it here; maybe we'll run into each other one evening.

DAY 2

Christianshavn, Government and Gardens

Christianshavn with its canals and the free community of Christiania, the government, Christiansborg Castle, art museum Ny Carlsberg Glyptoteket and dinner in the famous Tivoli Gardens (see map on pages 18–19 for route).

Relaxing at Christianshavn

– Make reservations for dinner in Tivoli (see below). Take bus No 2 or 8 from Rådhuspladsen or No 9 from Kongens Nytorv to the first stop in Christianshavn. –

Would you like to live in a quiet, yet lively traditional neighbourhood that is centrally located, has little traffic in the side streets, a waterfront promenade and a canal with sailing boats, plus a good number of restaurants and bars? Well, now you know why it is difficult to find an apartment in Christianshavn.

Christian IV planned Christianshavn in 1618 as part of his line of defence around Copenhagen. It started out as a naval base, and until a few years ago the navy still had its quarters at Holmen on the northeast side of Christianshavn. If you walk along **Strandgade**, the street facing the city, you'll find many houses from the 17th century still standing (look for the *anno domini* on the facade). The left side of the street is taken up by old warehouses that were once used for the storage of exotic imported goods, but now serve as government offices; further along is **Gammel Dok**, with exhibitions on Danish architecture and design.

When you cross the little bridge in Strandgade and walk around the block to the right, you will come to a boat-building yard on the canal. Until the 1930s the shipyard of Burmeister and Wain was located on this square, but they ran out of space and moved further out on Amager. Only small-scale industries have remained. The yellow house on the other side of the canal is **Søkvæsthuset**, with a library and a museum of naval history.

Cross the bridge again, turn left and then right at Wildersgade. **Café Wilder** and **Café Luna** on the corner of Sankt Annæ Gade are

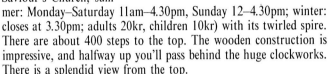

Vor Frelsers Kirke spire

two of the places that give the neighbourhood its special charm: at lunchtime, lawyers from the ministries based here share the cafes with people from the free community of Christiania. Everybody is welcome in Christianshavn.

Further up Sankt Annæ Gade on the other side of the Christianshavn canal you will find **Vor Frelsers Kirke** (Our Saviour's Church; summer: Monday–Saturday 11am–4.30pm, Sunday 12–4.30pm; winter: closes at 3.30pm; adults 20kr, children 10kr) with its twirled spire. There are about 400 steps to the top. The wooden construction is impressive, and halfway up you'll pass behind the huge clockworks. There is a splendid view from the top.

Around the corner in Prinsessegade, there used to be military barracks. But in 1971 a group of hippies jumped the fence around the abandoned buildings and proclaimed the area a free community. Thus **Christiania** (tours from main entrance daily 3pm) came into being, built on ideals of love, peace and brotherhood. In spite of police raids and several attempts from the government to normalise this social experiment, Christiania still survives. You are welcome to look around and maybe grab a bite to eat at one of the local cafes. The Christianites demand the freedom to live the way they like, build their houses according to their own needs and aesthetics, and also to smoke whatever they like, including pot. Hard drugs have been banned by the residents, but there is a busy market for marijuana in **Pusher Street**. Cameras are definitely unwelcome, so you should avoid taking pictures. Get your camera out again when you reach the lake, where some of the residents have built their own homes using great imagination and craftsmanship.

Christiania

Turn left when you exit Christiania the way you came in, then left again on Bådsmandsstræde and right on the old Christianshavns Voldgade. Follow this street across Torvegade and back to the canal. When the weather is good, you can rent a boat on the corner of Torvegade and paddle around in the harbour and the canal (summer only, 45kr per hour). You can also do as the residents do and sit on the old wooden railings and enjoy a beer or a pastry from the bakery at **Christianshavns Torv** market. This could be the place for your lunch break.

At home in Christiania

From this square, any of the buses will take you back across Knippelsbro to Slotsholmen, and you get off at the first stop. **Holmens Kirke** (Monday–Saturday 9am–2pm) to your right is the church of seafarers and of the navy. Inside is a curious reminder of how the traders became rich enough to build their warehouses on Christianshavn: the font is decorated with figurines of Moors and is tall enough to be used for the christening of negro slaves. Two Danish admirals, Tordenskjold and Niels Juel, have been buried in sarcophagi in the side chapel.

Holmens Kirke is situated next to **Slotsholmen** (Castle Island), which has been the seat of the government since the days of Absalon. The castle (Christiansborg Slot) dominating the square is the fifth on these grounds; the first four were either consumed by fires or simply torn down. To experience the grandeur of the palace, find the door in the middle of the facade and walk through the building to the inner court. In the right wing, the Queen receives her guests on formal occasions, but when she does not occupy the reception rooms, the public can share in the splendour normally reserved for the privileged (May–September tours at 11am and 3pm daily; October–April on Tuesday, Thursday, Saturday and Sunday; adults 25kr, children 10kr). The left wing houses the parliament, the **Folketinget** (tours on Sundays 10am–4pm; also weekdays in summer). Debates are open to the public, but otherwise visitors are not welcome.

Continue into the grounds where the building to the left contains the **Museum of Royal Coaches** (Saturday and Sunday 2–4pm; adults 20kr, children 10kr). The old court theatre in the same building has been preserved since 1767, and now serves as a unique museum of theatre history (Wednesday 2–4pm, Sunday noon–4pm). To the left, there is a passage to the the Folketinget, and across from it another passage to **The National Library** (Monday–Saturday 10am–7pm; adults 30kr, children 10kr). The new extension, The Black Diamond (Den Sorte Diamant) is an architectural masterpiece, with a fantastic bookstore and a good cafe.

From the Folketinget, turn down Tøjhusgade. Continue over Frederiksholms Canal to H.C. Andersens Boulevard and Copenhagen's impressive art museum **Ny Carlsberg Glyptoteket** (Tuesday–Sunday 10am–4pm; adults 15kr, children free; no charge Wednesday and Sunday). If the name rings a bell, it is no coincidence. The Carlsberg Breweries have always supported the arts, and the Glyptoteket owns a world-class collection of Egyptian, Greek, Roman and Etruscan sculpture along with paintings and sculpture by Degas, Gauguin, Rodin and van Gogh. The rooms are centred around a peaceful winter garden.

The Glyptoteket stands next to one of the entrances to the world-famous **Tivoli Gardens** (April–mid-September: 11am–midnight; Friday and Saturday to 1am; adults 49kr, children 25kr; most rides 9kr, or booklet of 10 tickets for 68kr). Tivoli maintains its old-world charm, but has also changed with the times. Each season brings new additions to its offerings. Children come to ride the carousels, retired people just to sit and watch the flowers and the families. Pick up a free map of the gardens at the main entrance.

For dinner, eating in Tivoli can be a bland and expensive experience, but there are exceptions. My own favourite is **Færgekroen** on the lake (Tel: 33 12 94 12, reservations necessary). The fare is standard Danish food with *smørrebrød* and some hot dishes. There is a free playground nearby, where parents are welcome to park their children. Another popular restaurant is **Grøften**, behind the pantomime theatre (Tel: 33 12 11 25, reservations necessary). Do as the Danes do and order fresh shrimps on white bread and beer.

At dusk, when lights and lanterns add a touch of magic to the fountains and flower beds, Tivoli changes character. Then the adults by far outnumber the children. At midnight (or 1am) it's all over, but on Wednesday and Saturday, Tivoli says goodnight in style with a fireworks display at 11.45pm.

Night-time at the Tivoli Gardens

Morning Itineraries

3. Frederiksberg

Behind the scenes at the Royal Copenhagen porcelain factory and Carlsberg Breweries, with sidetrips to the romantic Frederiksberg Have and the Zoo.

Blue-fluted porcelain

— Bus No 1 or 14 will take you from Rådhuspladsen to Royal Copenhagen at Smallegade 45. Get off at Søndre Fasanvej, cross the road and walk 100m (110 yards) back the way you came. —

Every single piece of **Royal Copenhagen** porcelain is painted by hand. At the factory, you'll get to see how. The transformation of a simple white plate into a piece of art at the hands of one of their experienced painters is a fascinating process. No less interesting are the prices in the gift shop. Everything is slight 'seconds' with 30–40 percent off, but the flaws are hard to find. The tour of the factory is free and lasts about an hour (tours start on the hour 9–11am and 1–2pm).

Once you've done your tour, walk from the factory towards the city, but make a right turn at Andebakkesti (just before the first traffic lights) to get to the lovely **Frederiksberg Have**. Follow the lake to the left, then cross over the bridge and turn left. A Chinese pavilion, added in the romantic period of the early 19th century, sits on an island by itself. When you get to the fountain and Frederiksberg Castle (Slot) stands in front of you, turn left and make your way out to the main gate, turning left and then right at the first fork in the path. Across from the park lies the octagonal Frederiksberg Kirke. Despite its small size, the location ensures that it is much used for fashionable weddings.

Along Pile Allé, between the park and Vesterbrogade, you'll find a number of outdoor restaurants known as 'family gardens'. They serve traditional Danish *smørrebrød*, open sandwiches that should be savoured with beer and aquavit. But before lunch, you can also catch a glimpse of how the beer is produced at **Carlsberg Breweries** (visitor centre open 10am–4pm, closed Monday). Just continue uphill, stop where the road bends and turn left towards the elephant gate. You'll get to see the impressive old copper kettles for the malt and the just as impressive modern

Chinese pavilion, Frederiksberg Have

bottling hall with a capacity of 78,000 bottles per hour. And yes, they serve samples.

Thus uplifted, make your way back to one of the family gardens or go down Valby Langgade to **Bjælkehuset** in No 2. The restaurants all serve the same kind of food, just trust your instinct on which one to choose. No matter which one you prefer, the **Copenhagen Zoo** will be nearby (Roskildevej 32, 9am–6pm in summer, 9am–5pm in spring and autumn, and 9am–4pm in winter; adults 70 kr, children 35 kr).

The zoo has an acclaimed children's enclosure, where

Carlsberg's elephant gate

the young ones are allowed to pet the goats. Throughout the garden, they have the opportunity to measure their own abilities against those of the (very docile) animals. Pick up directions in the information office.

Buses 6 or 28 will take you back into town. If you have time, stop briefly at the **City Museum** (Københavns Bymuseum; May–September 10am–4pm; October–April 1–4pm; closed Tuesdays) near Vesterbros Torv at Vesterbrogade 59. From May to September, a ceramic model on the front lawn here shows Copenhagen as it looked in the 16th century – a mere village compared to the capital of today.

16th-century Copenhagen at the City Museum

4. Lyngby

Hiking, biking or sailing in the park areas around coastal Lyngby.

– Take the S-train towards Hillerød or Holte, get off at Lyngby station and exit towards Jernbanepladsen. Alternatively, rent a bike in central Copenhagen (see Practical Information); remember to buy a special train ticket for the bike. Boating (May–September): if you would like to rent a canoe, call 45 85 67 70 to reserve one in advance. You can also take a tour boat around the lakes. Bring swimsuits. –

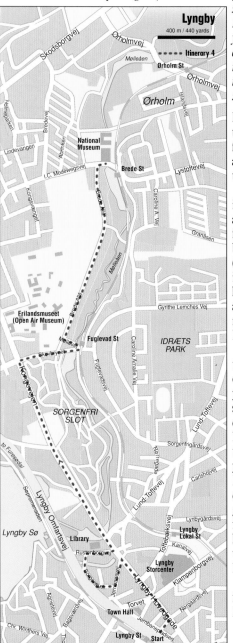

It takes just 20 minutes to get to Lyngby by train, but you'll feel like you are much further away from the hustle and bustle of the city.

At Frederiksdal Bådudlejning in Furesødal, you can rent a canoe by the hour, or for a full day. Bus 191 from Jernbanepladsen will take you there (get off where Nybrovej turns into Frederiksdalsvej). You'll have access to a couple of lakes and a brook, **Mølleåen**, which runs through **Dyrehaven** (the Deer Park).

If you don't want to do all the hard work yourself, boat-operators **Baadfarten** can take you around on the lakes instead. Proceed from the station down Jernbanevej, then make a left at Bagsværdvej and continue down Sorgenfrivej, where you'll find them at the bridge. For 70kr, you can buy an all-day ticket and sail across Lyngby and Bagsværd Lakes. Stop for an art exhibition at Sophienholm, or go for a walk in the woods – if you stay close to the lake, you can't lose your way.

If you prefer to hike or bike, follow Jernbanevej to Lyngby Hovedgade and turn left, pass

Canoeing on the Mølleåen

the church and enter the park a little further up to your right. You'll be headed north, and if you exit in the northwest corner, **Frilandsmuseet** (the Open Air Museum) is just 200m (650ft) up the road (Kongevejen 100; open Easter–October: Tuesday–Sunday 10am–5pm, October closes 4pm; adults 40kr, children free, Wednesdays free if space permits). Forty old farmhouses from around the country have been transplanted onto the grounds of this museum. The houses are still furnished, and although you're not allowed to touch anything, you can still get to feel what life was really like in the old days in Denmark.

When you leave, go back down Kongevejen, turn left at Skovbrynet and left again at Møllevej after the lake. Møllevej turns into Brede Allé, which will take you to the village of **Brede**, once an important centre for production of copperware, but nowadays known as the home of a department of the **National Museum** as well as for **Brede Gamle Spisehus**, a very good, moderately priced restaurant (Tel: 45 85 54 57; Tuesday–Sunday 11.30am–3pm and 5.30–10pm). The National Museum features two permanent exhibits: one is about the history of Mølleåen, the other about clothing and body culture (Tuesday–Sunday 10am–5pm; free).

If you are tired of walking, catch the train back to Jægersborg S-train station. You can also walk on to the next stop in Ørholm. Bikes are not allowed on this particular train, so tired bikers will simply have to turn around and return to Lyngby, or ride the 7km (4¼ mile) to Klampenborg Station on the coast – left on Modewegsvej, then immediately right into the woods again, across Ørholmvej, left when you cross the railroad tracks, then right (follow the signs towards Strandmøllen and Klampenborg) and right again at Krudtmøllestien; when you get to the paved road in Rådvad, turn left

Farmhouse furnishings, Frilandmuseet

A pastoral scene, Mølleåen

and go through the village, then turn left up Chauseen and stay on that trail the rest of the way. You'll get a good view of the sea, and you should also be able to see some of the long-legged creatures that have given the Deer Park its name. The roads are somewhat hilly, so you'll deserve a drink at **Peter Lieps Hus** (tel: 39 64 07 86) or in the **Bakken** amusement park, once you've finished this 12km (7 mile) tour – *see page 39 for more on Klampenborg.*

Afternoon Itineraries

5. The Old Ramparts

A stroll through the parks of Copenhagen with side trips to nearby art museums.

– Take the S-train, or buses 5, 14 or 16 to Nørreport Station. –

Copenhagen is praised as a green city – thanks to Christian IV. His many wars with the Swedes and the Germans forced him to think about its defence, and as a precaution, he planned a ring of ramparts and moats all the way around it. Although the circle has been broken in some places, you can still follow most of it through Tivoli, Ørstedsparken, Botanisk Have and Øster Anlæg to the Citadel in the north, and even across the harbour to Christiania. Start at the **Botanical Garden** (Botanisk Have), where every tree or shrub has a little name-tag attached. I rarely study them, but I like the garden for its variety and the beautiful greenhouse full of tropical plants (daily 10am–3pm; no charge). At the end of the garden, cross the road to get to the next park, **Østre Anlæg**. You'll still be following the old moat: the large red building to the right is **The**

The Botanical Garden

36

In the Kunstindustrimuseet

State Museum of Art (Statens Museum for Kunst) with collections of Danish artists and an excellent modern art extension (Tuesday–Sunday 10am–5pm; adults 40kr, children free, Wednesday free).

The smaller classical building to the left is **Hirschsprung's Collection** with its impressive display of Danish paintings from the golden age of the 19th and early 20th century (Thursday–Monday 10am–4pm, Wednesday until 9pm; adults 25kr, children free).

When you exit Østre Anlæg, turn right on Oslo Plads and cross the railway tracks, then head for **Nyboder**, the low yellow buildings in front. These are some of the quarters that Christian IV built for his marine soldiers, and even today they are rented exclusively to naval officers. Other military quarters are found at the **Citadel** in the park on the other side of Grønningen. Christian IV had left his line of ramparts unfinished when it reached the water, but his son Frederik III finished the work for him by creating the Citadel with five bastions and a double moat. Follow the moat to the entrance and walk straight towards the central square. The area is still a military reservation, so access is restricted. There is, however, one place where everybody can come; the library to the left of the church (on the first floor through the building and the garden).

If you scale the bastion behind the church, you'll see a Dutch windmill, where all the corn for the military bakery used to be ground. The mill is still tested once a year, on the Citadel's

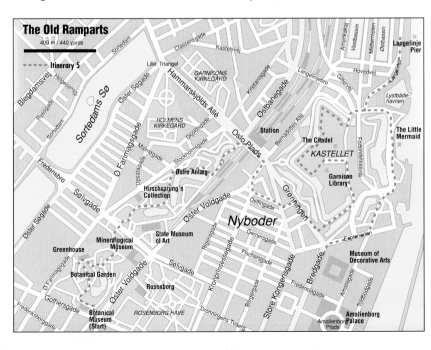

anniversary, 28 October. Follow the path to the last bastion and exit towards the north. A staircase leads up to the road. Turn right and walk towards the marina between **Langelinje Pier** and the *Little Mermaid*. Hans Christian Andersen's touching story about the mermaid who fell in love with a human prince and gave her voice in exchange for a pair of legs, only to see her loved one marry someone else, inspired the artist Edvard Eriksen. The statue is the trademark for the Danish tourist organizations.

To get back to the city, you can catch bus No. 29 from the Langelinie Promenade. Consider making a detour to **Kunstindustrimuseet** (the Museum of Decorative Arts) in Bredgade 68 with both medieval and modern design works (Tuesday–Friday 10am–4pm, Saturday–Sunday 12–4pm; adults 35kr, children free). Built around a garden, the museum makes an appropriate last stop on a tour of the parks.

6. Hellerup and Klampenborg

This itinerary will appeal to the whole family: it includes the Experimentarium (Science Centre), Denmark's Aquarium, a trip to the beach and to the Bakken amusement park.

The Experimentarium, where science is fun

– Take the S-train or bus No. 6 or 21 from Rådhuspladsen/Kongens Nytorv to Tuborgvej in Hellerup. The Experimentarium is located in the buildings of Tuborg Breweries. Bring swimsuits. –

Did you hate physics in school? Then the **Experimentarium** will show you a couple of really cool things the teacher forgot to tell you about (daily

On Bellevue Beach

10am–5pm June–August; otherwise, hours vary slightly; adults 85kr, children 60kr). You can watch, touch and test some of the stranger phenomena of sound and light, dance in a discotheque where the music follows your movements, study your own skeleton and much more. It's hard to tell who gets more excited, the kids or their parents.

Continue on bus 6 to **Charlottenlund Fort**. On the water side, you'll have a white sand beach, a large lawn and the ruins of a former military stronghold. To the other side lie the woods and **Denmark's Aquarium**, where you can study electric eels and other strange varieties of fish and shellfish (February–September: 10am–6pm, November–January: 10am–4pm; adults 60kr, children 30kr; the fish get fed on Thursday and Sunday at 2pm). All in all, you can't find a better place to let the children loose with safety. There are also sufficient numbers of ice-cream vendors and hot dog stands plus a nice little circular cafe and sandwich bar.

Dyrehaven coachman

A similar piece of paradise lies 3.5km (2¼ miles) down the road. Get back on bus 6 to Klampenborg, where you'll have **Bellevue Beach** across from **Dyrehaven** (The Deer Park), and **Bakken** amusement park close by (just follow the signs). Bakken, which is reputedly the world's oldest amusement park, isn't quite as charming as Tivoli, but there is no entrance charge and four times as many amusements to try, ranging from water-slides to the traditional House of Horrors (rides cost around 15kr, or 5kr for children). For dinner try Peter Lieps Hus, a few minutes' walk to the north, serving *smørrebrod* and other Danish specialities.

Excursions from Copenhagen

Kronborg Castle and the old merchants' houses, with side trips to the Science Museum, Louisiana Museum of Modern Art and even to Sweden.

– The Copenhagen Card will save you money on this trip. Make reservations for dinner (see below). Trains leave from the central railway station three times an hour. When you come out of Helsingør Station, you'll see Kronborg Castle in front of you, a 10–15 minute walk away. –

Helsingør is situated at the entrance to the Øresund, the narrow belt of water that separates Denmark from Sweden. For centuries, the city thrived because it could claim dues from all ships passing through the belt. **Kronborg Castle** was erected around 1420 to ensure that the captains would pay their dues, with cannons pointing out over the water, and later modernised and expanded to the impressive Renaissance castle of today. Shakespeare found Kronborg an enticing backdrop for prince Hamlet to ponder the essential questions of life and death, and the Danes also claim that legendary Viking chief Holger Danske, who is sitting asleep in the cellar, will come to their rescue if the nation is ever in dire need. Most of the castle is open, including the ballroom, the church and the dark dungeon (May–September: daily 10.30am–5pm; winter 11am–3pm, closed Monday; adults 40kr, children 15kr). The castle is also the site of the Danish Maritime Museum (same hours as castle; adults 40kr, children 20kr) If you are travelling with children, you should also consider a visit to **Teknisk Museum** (the Science Museum), with its displays of machines and inventions from the past three centuries. Take a taxi or bus 340 to Nordre Strandvej 23 (Tuesday–Sunday 10am–5pm; adults 25kr, children 15kr).

Kronborg Castle, inspiration for 'Hamlet'

If you need a coffee break when you get back to the harbour area, try **Kammercafeen** in the former customs building behind the tourist information office (from where you can get a free city map). The staff can also help you in case you'd like to stay overnight and maybe spend the next day on the beautiful Hornbæk Beach nearby.

Finding your way around Helsingør is not at all difficult. The

The famous ice-cream of Brostræde

city is laid out in a rectangle formed by the three pedestrian streets and Axeltorv Square. During shopping hours it is always busy. A return ticket across the sound to Helsingborg, Sweden, costs 35 kr, and ferries depart every 20 minutes, allowing Swedes to pop across for cheaper grocery shopping. But before you start mixing with our Scandinavian neighbours, you should see a bit of the old Helsingør.

From the tourist office, walk left along the alley of Brostræde (famous for its ice-cream cones). Just two house numbers to the right, you'll find the even narrower Gammel Færgestræde, where you can get an idea of what Helsingør looked like some 400 years ago. Cross Stengade and continue up Sanct Annagade, where **Sankt Olai Kirke** will soon appear to your right (Monday–Friday 10am–2pm, May–August until 4pm). The church dates back to 1559, but the wall on the left of the entrance also carried the first church on the grounds, as far back as 1230. Notice the frescoes above the pulpit, typical of Danish churches from the Middle Ages. The christening chapel in the southwest corner is as old as the church, but the paintings of the apostles were added later.

When you come out, cross the street and follow Skt Olai Gade all the way to the end, then turn left. Between Nos 7 and 9, Munkegade starts. Follow it one block, then turn left, and you'll come to Stengade, the main pedestrian street. If you are not into shopping, just continue down Skyttenstræde to Strandgade. The oldest private house in Helsingør is situated at No 27, half-timbered and erected in 1577. Strandgade will lead you back to the station.

Old Helsingør

About 8km (5 miles) south of Helsingør lies the **Louisiana Museum of Modern Art** (Gl. Strandvej 13, daily 10am–5pm, to 10pm on Wednesday; adults 60 kr, children 20 kr). An outstanding collection of Henry Moore, Calder, Giacometti, Max Ernst etc, has made Louisiana the most visited art museum in the country. The architecture itself is an attraction, with a fine view of the water from the buildings, which are connected by a beautiful park. (Take the train to Humlebæk and follow the signs through the woods; the museum is 1km north of the station.)

South of Louisiana lies the old hamlet of **Sletten**. Turn left when you leave Louisiana and follow Gammel Strandvej along the water. If you'd like to get back to Copenhagen, turn right on Oscar Bruunsvej to get to the train station. But if you'd like to stay for dinner, follow the twisting Gl. Strandvej until you get to **Sletten Kro** at No 137. It's pricey, but worth the money. You can also make a right turn, walk up to Strandvejen, catch bus 388 towards Lyngby and ride along the pretty coastline to Tårbæk, where you can dine at **Tårbæk Kro** with a nice view of the old marina. Bus 388 continues to Klampenborg Station (a 15–20 minute walk).

8. Roskilde

To the Church of the Kings, with side trips to the Viking Ship Museum, Ledreborg Palace and the Archaeological Research Centre in Lejre.

– The Copenhagen Card will save you money on this trip. Frequent trains leave from the central railway station. In Roskilde, follow the signs towards 'Domkirken' or the tourist information. –

The **cathedral** (Domkirken) or Church of the Kings rises majestically above the hills and the fjord of Roskilde, reminding visitors that this is a city of importance. When Copenhagen was still a

The Harbour | The Viking Ship Museum

Roskilde

400 m / 440 yards

- - - - Itinerary 8

St Jørgensbjerg Church

Brøndgade · Havnevej · Skt Ibs Vej · St Ibs Church · Strandengen · Skt Agnes Vej · Kong Knud den Stores Vej · Kong Valdemars Vej · Kongebakken

Sankt Claravej · Frederiksborgvej · Kloster buen · Roskilde Park · Klosterengen · Dronning Margrethes Vej

Sankt Mortens Vej · Rovstesfræde · Roskilde Cathedral · Start · Dronning Margrethes Vej

Villavej · Maglekildevej · Bondetinget · Roskilde Museum · Algade · Heste Torvet · Østergade

Lützhøfts Merchant's House · Skomagergade · The Palace Collections · Market · Skt. Ols Strǽde

Borgediget · Ringstedgade · Schmeltz Plads · Bredgade · Allehelgensgade · Grønne Gade · Grønnegade · Østergade

The Church of Our Lady · Jernbanegade

---

hamlet among many others, Roskilde was the capital of Denmark and one of the largest cities in Northern Europe. But ironically, the cathedral was founded at the same time as Absalon built his first castle in Copenhagen, and Roskilde has never regained the status it had.

Since 1423, the cathedral has been the burial place for the kings and queens of Denmark. This tradition was initiated by Queen Margrethe I, whose body lies in a marble sarcophagus behind the altar. New side chapels were added whenever space was needed. In 1985, Frederik IX was laid to rest behind the church; his wife, Queen Ingrid, was buried here in 2000. The cathedral is open to the public most of the time (tel: 46 35 16 24 to inquire about opening hours; adults 15kr, children 10kr).

If you didn't see the Viking exhibit at the National Museum, you should consider a trip to the **Viking Ship Museum** (Vikingeskibsmuseet) at Roskilde Fjord (May–October: daily 9am–5pm, November–April: daily 10am–4pm; adults 54kr, children 30kr). To get there, walk down through the park behind the cathedral to Sankt Claravej. On the way, you'll pass Sankt Hans Spring, where you can get a refreshing drink of cool water. The museum contains five ships that were recovered from the bottom of the fjord in 1962 plus a modern, full-size model and information on the technology of the Vikings. But don't get too excited: all that remains of the actual ships are some charred beams.

Roskilde is full of students

Proceed from the museum to the harbour and turn left up the stairs to **Sankt Jørgensbjerg**, the old part of town. Follow Kirkegade, Asylgade and Sankt Hansgade back to the cathedral. If you walk south from the cathedral to the market square and turn left onto Algade, you'll find an excellent bakery called Den Gamle Bagergård on the right.

Roskilde Cathedral

Once you've seen enough of Roskilde, walk back to the station in time to catch the train leaving for Holbæk. The first stop is Lejre Station, where bus 233 will be waiting to take you to the **Historical Archaeological Research Centre** (Lejre Forsøgcenter; May–October daily 10am–5pm; adults 60kr, children 30kr), situated here because Lejre was a central town in the early history of Denmark. You shouldn't be put off by the centre's name – its approach to the study of history is practical: every summer, selected families stay here for a week and try to live life as they did in the Iron Age or in the 19th century. As a visitor, you can follow them around, or even try to grind your own corn, or sail in a hollowed oak at the activity centre.

This part of the tour will be a hit with children, but at the next stop at **Ledreborg Palace** (June–August daily 11am–5pm; access to the park all year; adults 50kr, children 25kr) they must respect the usual 'do not touch' commands. The palace is an easy 2km (1 mile) walk from the Archaeological Centre, or you can take bus 233, linking Roskilde, the Archaeological Centre and Ledreborg.

At the research centre you got a glimpse of ordinary people's lives; Ledreborg will show you the much more elegant lifestyle of the aristocracy. Built by Count Johan Ludvig von Holstein around 1750, the palace still belongs to the Holstein family. The strict symmetry of the Versailles-style park and buildings is impressive. In the basement is the dungeon and the old kitchen, which was still being used as late as 1950.

If you don't want to wait for the bus, you can walk back to Lejre railway station through the park (ask for directions).

Simulating the Iron Age at the Research Centre

ÅRHUS & AROUND

Itineraries in Jutland

9. Århus

Through the Old Town museum and the actual old town of Århus, with stops at medieval churches and modern cafés.

– Pick up a copy of the monthly What's on in Århus *and a city map at the tourist information office in the town hall building; the staff can also tell you about tourist tickets for the buses. The Old Town is paved with cobblestones, so leave your high-heeled shoes at the hotel. Bus 3 towards Hasle runs from the town hall to the Old Town. Arrive before 10am to beat the crowds. –*

Jutland's capital city is Århus, a lively "college town" known for its music, theatre, ballet, art and cafes, as well as its fun Festival Week every autumn. Denmark's second largest city – with a population of about 280,000, only a fraction of Copenhagen's – this harbour town is noted for its nearby forests, beaches and castles. It seems like every kiosk in Denmark sells stacks of pretty postcards

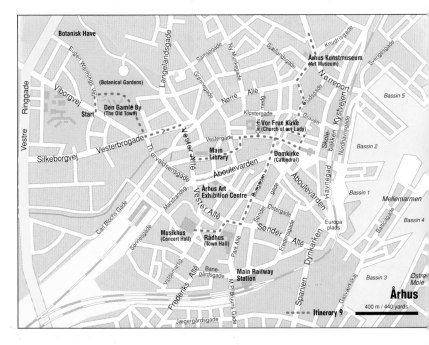

The Old Town of Århus

with pictures of quaint village idylls. The **Old Town** (Den Gamle By) is just such an idyll (Tel: 86 12 31 88; June–August daily 9am–6pm; September–May hours vary; adults 60kr, children 15kr; you'll need a 20kr brochure with a map). The only difference is that this is not a town but a museum, comprising 75 restored houses from all around the country dating from the Renaissance to World War I.

The school came from Funen, the post office from North Jutland, the pharmacy from South Jutland, and so forth. None of the buildings are inhabited, but they are all open, so you can see how they used to be furnished. Each house represents a different trade: the hatter, the potter, the printer, the brewer, the tailor, the baker. At the bakery, you can buy fresh sugar-sprinkled pringles and other goodies. If you would like a cup of coffee with them, there is also a nice restaurant, **Simonsens Have**, where you are allowed to bring your own food (as long as you buy a drink). There are classical concerts in the yard on summer Sundays.

When you exit, walk back towards the city alongside the town museum through the Botanical Garden. Turn left at Vesterbrogade and then right at Vesterbros Allé, then left again when you reach the park area. The large building to your left is the public library (they have foreign newspapers in the reading room). Continue down the narrow Møllestien and turn left where it ends, then right on Vestergade to get to **Vor Frue Kirke** (Church of Our Lady; Monday–Friday 10am–2pm, Saturday 10am–noon). The church once belonged to a monastery, and the old buildings are still standing. Like so many other monasteries, it survived the Reformation only because of its usefulness as a hospital for the poor. The complex dates back to around 1250, but during renovation in the mid-1950s an even older church was discovered below the present one. This crypt church was reconsecrated and is now back in use again.

Just 300m (330 yards) down the street, the **Domkirken**, the

Bakery, the Old Town

A cheerful visitor

Cathedral of St Clement (summer 9.30am–4pm, winter 10am–3pm) presides over Store Torv, the main square. Built in the early 13th century by bricklayers trained in southern Europe, it is the largest in the country. For a Lutheran church, it is richly decorated: the frescoes in the ceiling are outstanding, as are the Renaissance pulpit, the Dutch font, and the many memorial tablets on the walls. The pointed spire offers one of the best views of the city from its belfry.

The area north of the cathedral is so full of cafes that choosing one is difficult. They all serve good food, most of them at low prices. Try the streets around Volden, Graven, Klostergade and Studsgade for their variety of ethnic food, from Middle Eastern to French. The cafes share the neighbourhood with lots of little shops – no hardware stores or auto part dealers, just lots of clothes, records, art and antiques.

An option for the afternoon is **Århus Kunstmuseum** (Museum of Art; 10am–5pm, Wednesday until 8pm; adults 40kr, children free), which has a good collection of Danish paintings from the past two centuries and is quick to pick up on emerging trends in the art world. The museum lies in the south corner of Århus University campus. Århus has a student population of around 40,000 during term time, which gives the town a lively, youthful atmosphere.

Walk back to the cathedral and up the pedestrian shopping mall,

In the Café Casablanca

or catch a bus (No 1, 11 or 14) back to the town hall (Rådhuset). On the other side of the square you'll find the **Concert Hall** (Musik huset), a modern glass house with three large concert halls. The Hall is open every night, so pick up a schedule at the ticket office. It is also the home of the Danish National Opera, which has made marathon performances of Strauss and Wagner a summer tradition. Musikhuset is also a focal point for Århus Festuge, a festival that brings the whole city to its feet in the first week of September (tel. 89 31 82 70; www.aarhusfestuge.dk).

The nightlife and the restaurants in Århus are centred around Skolegade, the cafe district, and Vestergade behind the cathedral. A few bars are centred around Jægergårdsgade behind the train station. Look for inspiration in the *Nightlife* chapter.

Excursions from Århus

10. Silkeborg

To the beautiful lake country around Silkeborg, to the west of Århus, plus visits to the art museum and the Tollund Man. By paddle-steamer to Sky Mountain (Himmelbjerget).

– Drive or take the train from Århus to Silkeborg. If you like, you can easily reverse the itinerary by starting in Ry. If you are travelling with children, who might not enjoy 2½ hours on a boat, there is also a one-hour cruise on the lakes from Silkeborg. –

Silkeborg lies in one of the areas where the Danes go to spend their summer vacations. The country between Silkeborg and Skanderborg is as beautiful as can be. Criss-crossed by quiet rivers, it provides the ideal setting for canoeing or hiking trips, or just for lazy days spent in the sun with a picnic basket. A couple of first-class museums in Silkeborg finish the picture off.

From Silkeborg train station walk down Estrupsgade to Skoletorvet, where you'll find **Galerie Moderne** (Monday–Saturday 10am–5pm; free) at No 39. Don't be fooled by the surroundings – it is one of the best galleries in Denmark, specialising in modern, abstract art by people such as Corneille and Alechinsky plus some of the top names in Denmark: Asger Jorn, Peter Brandes and many others. If you like what you see, there is more at the **Silkeborg Art Museum** (Tuesday–Friday noon–4pm, weekends 10am–5pm; adults 30kr, children free). Walk back towards the station and turn left on Drewsensvej; when it turns into a path, follow it for one more block, then turn right at Åhavevej and continue past the canoe rental shops to Åhave Allé. The museum stands on top of the hill.

To catch up with the rest of the itinerary, just stay on Åhavevej when you walk back.

If abstract art is not your cup of tea, ignore the Galerie Moderne and

Tollund Man

take the first right from Skoletorvet and walk all the way down Nygade; **Café Picasso** on the intersecting Tværgade is a nice place to stop for something to drink or a freshly made sandwich. Turn left on Søndergade, which will take you to the town hall square; turn right and walk down the passage on the right side of the church. The **Silkeborg Museum** of local history (summer daily 10am–5pm, winter Wednesday and weekends noon–4pm; adults: 20kr, children: 5kr) lies on the other side of Christian VIII's Vej. Here again, Silkeborg has a first-rate sight hidden behind a local label: the **Tollund Man** is the remarkably well-preserved body of a man who died about 2,200 years ago. A rope around his neck shows that he was hanged before he was thrown into a bog. The acidic peat served as a natural defence against decay. When he was found, a young boy had been reported missing, and the police were called in to check the body. However, the peat above him was compact and had not been touched for centuries. His face is so lifelike that you can see even the stubble on his chin. He looks relaxed and at ease, as if he is just sleeping.

Tower of Himmelbjerget

The museum lies close to the water, from where you can rent a canoe or take a tour boat out on Julsø Lake. The most famous of the boats is *Hjejlen* (The Plover), which has been sailing on the lake since 1861. It is the oldest paddle steamer still in use in the world, and it will take you on an unforgettable cruise to **Himmelbjerget**. *Hjejlen* sails only twice a day (10am and 1.45pm, July and August only), and you have to be there at least half an hour in advance, since they don't take reservations (there are other boats than *Hjejlen* that don't fill up as quickly). The trip takes 1 hour and 15 minutes each way and allows you one hour on Himmelbjerget; you can have lunch on board if you wish.

Himmelbjerget translates as the Sky Mountain. A slight exaggeration, perhaps, because although this is one of the highest peaks in the country, it reaches just 147m (482ft) above sea level. But look at it this way: scaling a hill this size is not difficult, and the view from the top is magnificent.

There is a beautiful 7km (4¼ mile) trail to the small town of Ry through the woods. If you don't want to go back the way you came, you can also take the boat back to Ry and the train to Århus from there. But perhaps you noticed the good restaurants in Silkeborg's Nygade. **Café Piaf** at No 31 offers good, French food at moderate prices. Afterwards, you can sit outside at **Musikværkstedet** (No 18, in the backyard) and listen to jazz or folk music.

The 'Hjejlen' has been sailing since 1861

11. Djursland

Along country roads north of Århus to manor houses, Stone Age monuments and old farming and fishing villages.

– This excursion is planned for those who are driving, but you can also get to most of the places by bus: the last paragraph will tell you how. –

The beautiful peninsula of Djursland, with its varied landscape of moorland, woods, hills and beaches, lies just half an hour's drive north of Århus.

Djursland has always been a popular place. You turn a corner, and a 4,000-year-old grave mound appears out in a field. Just a few kilometres further away it might be a Renaissance manor house that greets you. And on the way from one sight to the next you will pass through charming little villages with 13th-century Romanesque churches and 17th-century farmhouses.

Driving up from Århus, stay off the freeway and follow the Daisy-route from Skæring (a Daisy-booklet is available at most bookstores). As soon as you have passed through Hornslet, **Rosenholm Castle** (Slot) will appear on your left (June–August daily 11am–4pm; May and September weekends only; adults 60kr, children 30kr). Built in 1559, in part with bricks from nearby Kalø Castle, Rosenholm is one of the finest Renaissance castles in the country, complete with a moat, towers and a beautiful park with peacocks.

Stay on the Daisy-route. It continues through Mørke and Rønde

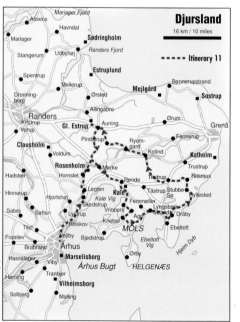

to **Mols Bjerge**, where it will take you through the villages of Vrinners, Agri, Knebel, and Vistoft – strange names, even to a Danish ear. Between Agri and Knebel, look for **Posekjær Stenhus**, a large round Stone Age cairn. The outer ring of rocks supposedly keeps evil spirits away. There were originally three graves in the middle; that's why the remaining one appears to be off-centre.

Some of the farms here sell their own produce from stalls along the road. Often each stall is nothing more than a shelf with an empty jar serving as the cash register. The

The hill country of Mols Bjerge

prices are listed on a piece of cardboard, and you just help yourself to the cherries *(kirsebær)*, berries *(bær)*, apples *(æbler)*, pears *(pærer)*, peas *(ærter)*, carrots *(gulerødder)* or whatever is in season, and leave exact change.

Do not turn left inland, but stay on the road along the coast following the Daisy-route until you get into **Ebeltoft**. There are a couple of parking areas next to the post office on the waterside, and the pedestrian street is just one block away from the water. Ebeltoft is a lovely old town, but this is no secret, so on a good summer's day there will be thousands of people here. However, it is easy to get away from the crowds: once you have gone through the centre, just stay on the south side of the central square. If you would like to know more about Ebeltoft, pick up the free tourist brochure in the old town hall. On Saturdays, this building is still used for weddings. For lunch in Ebeltoft, the restaurant **Mellem Jyder** at the beginning of Juulsbakke has the kind of old-fashioned provincial ambience that the cafes rebel against.

Exit the old part of town through Toldbodgade (off Juulsbakke). The

Posekjær Stenhus, a Stone Age cairn

yellow house at the end of the street is the **Glasmuseet**, (Strandvejen 8; July daily 10am–9pm, all other months daily 10am–5pm; adults 40kr, children 5kr) a unique museum of modern glassworks. Five hundred artists from different countries have submitted some of their best works, and the museum has such a large collection of glass sculpture that it has to change the exhibition frequently in order to do justice to all the artists. They have glass kites, glass portrait busts and other unusual items.

About 200m (220yds) to the right, *Fregatten Jylland (Frigate Jutland)* has undergone extensive restoration. She was built in 1860 as the largest wooden ship of the navy and has cruised as far

Rosenholm Castle

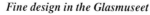
Fine design in the Glasmuseet

away as the West Indies. Although she was a good sailor and did well in a fight with the Prussians in 1864, she has long since been retired. Restoration was completed in 1996, and it is possible to get on board and study her construction first hand (Strand-vejen 4; daily; July–August 9am–7pm; April–June and September–October 10am–5pm; November–March 10am–4pm; adults 60kr, children 20kr).

Leaving Ebeltoft to the north catch the Daisy-route again and turn right towards **Dråby**. The village church is unusually large and spacious and is beautifully decorated with frescoes. **Hyllested Church** also has frescoes but of an earlier and much more frivolous kind: Adam and Eve are portrayed embarrassedly clutching their fig leaves, but the painter didn't give the devil similar protection.

From Hyllested you can continue to Rosmus and turn left to-wards Tirstrup, where you'll hit the main road back to Århus. But if the day is still young and you would like to see some more, turn right a few kilometres after Tirstrup and follow the signs towards Kolind and Ryomgård. Stay on the road until you get to Auning (via Pindstrup), then turn left. On the other side of Auning you'll soon see the impressive structure of the **Gammel Estrup** manor house (April–October daily 10am–5pm; November–March Tues-day–Sunday 10am–4pm; adults 65kr, children free). The interiors are not quite as extravagant as those at Rosenholm, but still worth seeing. The **Museum of Agriculture** (same hours as manor house), located in the farm buildings, adds an interesting contrast. It shows just how much hard work it took to survive in the country in the old days. You can see the tools used 200 years ago, and a contem-porary farmer's kitchen is pitted against the kitchens of 100 and 200 years ago. The museum shows how hard-working farm labour-ers have been substituted by machines, both inside their buildings and outside.

To get back to Århus at the end of this long day, turn right in Auning and follow road 563. You'll get back on to the Daisy-route south of Hvilsager, this time travelling towards Århus. If us-ing **Public Transport**, catch bus 123 to Ebeltoft, leaving from the coach terminal in Århus (regular departures Monday–Friday). When you have seen Ebeltoft, consider a trip through Mols Bjerge on a local bus – routes 1 and 2 from Ebeltoft's bus terminal will take you past the Posekjær Cairn. Alternatively take bus 123 to Femmoller and walk down to the sea from here. If you like, get off at the main stop in Knebel and stroll down to the water, until the bus comes back half an hour later. Alternatively, you can take Nos 119 or 214 from Århus to Rosenholm Castle and either continue to Gammel Estrup two hours later or go back to Løgten, where you can change to bus 123 to Ebeltoft. Call 86 12 67 03 to verify times. There are no bus services further south in the Mols peninsula.

NORTH JUTLAND

12. Skagen

The art museums of Skagen followed by lunch on the wharf, then a visit to the open-air museum in Skagen Vesterby, and finally to Grenen, the tip of Jutland. Finish on a fine beach.

– If you rent a bicycle (see Practical Information) Skagen to Grenen is no distance, but if you walk I recommend that you visit the museums and Grenen on one day and save Vesterby and the sand-buried church for the next. That will give you two half days to spend on the beach. –

Skagen's claim to fame is not just that it lies at the very tip of Jutland, where the land nose-dives into the sea. The town would be an attraction in itself, even if nature had been less intriguing. With its charming yellow houses and white picket fences, Skagen is just as picturesque as Ebeltoft or Helsingør. In addition, some of the best Danish painters of the late 19th century settled in Skagen, among them P.S. Krøyer and Michael and Anna Ancher, whose style is often labelled as Scandinavian impressionism. Some people come to Skagen just to visit the local art museum and see the magical Scandinavian light.

From the train station, walk up Sct Laurentii Vej (towards Grenen) until you see a sign for Brøndums Hotel on your right. **Skagen Museum** is located on this road, and the museum gives a good introduction to life on Skagen (Brøndumsvej 4, tel: 98 44 64 44; June–August daily 10am–6pm; May and September daily 10am–5pm; times vary during the rest of year; adults 50kr, children free). Whether it is a painting of Marie Krøyer and Anna Ancher walking on the beach at sunset or of fishermen dragging a boat onshore, these works portray situations that can still be seen,

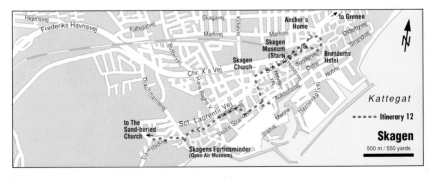

Picturesque Skagen, at the tip of Jutland

even if people doing such things today don't wear the same clothes as they do in the paintings.

The artists used to meet at **Brøndums Hotel**, and you should also treat yourself to a cup of coffee here while you watch people go by. Anna and Michael Ancher lived close by, and you can retrace their steps from the hotel through the neighbourhood to their **house** at Markvej 2. Walk around the hotel and follow Østerbygade, then take the first side street to the left. When you reach the end of the street, walk towards the water tower and you'll be there (July–August daily 10am–6pm; May, June and September daily 10am–5pm; April and October daily 11am–3pm; November–March weekends only 11am–3pm; adults 40kr, children 10kr). The house was originally more sparsely furnished than it is now, but the style is the same. There are paintings everywhere, and even the door frames have been decorated with pretty flowers.

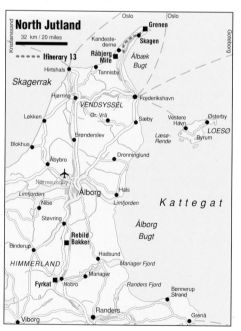

Follow Sct Laurentii Vej back, then turn right on Kappelgangen to get to **Skagen Church**. The church has been renovated and provides a peaceful break from the busy streets. Just about every church near the coast has ship models hanging from the ceiling, as here. They were put up by fishermen wishing for calm weather and a safe return.

Skagen's sand-buried church

Fishing is still an important trade in Skagen, and most of the harbour area is reserved for storage or transportation companies. But there is a large marina in the centre, which is where half the town gathers at lunchtime. To get there, walk across Sct Laurentii Vej and continue down Trondsvej. Most people buy a tray with fishcakes, smoked herring, fried squid or some other fish-based dish from one of the little shops, but you can also sit down at **Skagen Fiskerestaurant.** If you sit outside there is self-service from the counter, but upstairs in the main building you order from the menu or serve yourself from the herring buffet.

When you leave the harbour, find Vesterbyvej (it runs parallel to Sct Laurentii Vej). This street turns into Svallerbakken, which ends at **Skagen By og Egnsmuseum**, the open-air museum of local history (P.K. Nielsensvej; May–September: 10am–5pm, weekends 11am–5pm; March–April and October–November Monday–Friday 10am–4pm; adults 30kr, children 5kr). There's a striking contrast here between the house of a wealthy fisherman and that of his poor colleague, who lived with his parents, his wife and six children in just one room. The museum also shows how Skagen has changed over the years, from a village of black wooden buildings to the yellow and red brick houses of today. One of the halls is dedicated to the many men, both young and old, who never came back from sea.

About 1km (½ mile) further south, you'll find one of the eeriest reminders of Skagen's struggle with nature. Out in the middle of the woods, a lonesome church tower rises between the trees. When you get closer, it turns out that there is nothing left but the tower. The church, **Den Tilsandede Kirke**, was erected in the 14th century at a safe distance from the beach, but the sand kept moving closer, and by the late 18th century, the parishioners had to dig their way to church. In 1795, they finally gave up and tore down the main building, but they left the tower standing (June–August 11am–5pm; adults 8kr, children 4kr). The trees in the area have been planted to keep the sand from drifting any further. Walk down Gammel Kirkesti (across Damstedvej), where you'll see the forlorn tower in the distance.

Ocean wrestling at Grenen

Damstedvej leads down to a really nice beach, less crowded than its counterpart north of Skagen. But if you don't have your swimsuit with you, you should head all the way up north to

Grenen for a spectacular view of the sea instead. At the tip of Jutland, Kattegat wrestles with the North Sea, and it looks like an even fight. You can stand with one foot in each, but be careful, because the current is strong. (Swimming is prohibited here, as it is extremely dangerous.)

A bus leaves for Grenen from the train station in summer, but it is also within walking distance (4km/2½ miles from the south end of Skagen, 2km from the north end). Just before you reach Grenen you can get a great view of the whole area from the top of the lighthouse. Grenen is always popular, but is never more so than around sunset, the local rush hour.

On Råbjerg Mile, a travelling dune

13. Kandestederne

Swimming in the west coast surf near Skagen, with lunch at the romantic Hjorths Hotel, then past a travelling sand dune to Gammel Skagen.

— Bring swimming gear. During the high season, bus No 99 leaves from the railway station at irregular intervals (ask for a schedule at the train station). Get off in Kandestederne (a 25-minute ride). —

Skagerrak is a docile sea compared to its neighbour on the west coast. The beaches of Skagen town are pleasant, but you shouldn't leave North Jutland without a taste of the North Sea waves. **Kandestederne** is one of the best beaches to visit. Don't expect beach chairs and cocktail waitresses, because here you'll only find a flat white sand beach and the powerful west-coast surf. In Kandestederne, nature provides free entertainment for those who like to ride the waves and get their faces wet. It is not the best place to bring small children, but a 5 or 6-year-old should be able to hold his own against the waves, and enjoy it too.

Kandestederne has another advantage: when you get tired of playing, you can put your clothes back on and walk a few hundred meters up to **Hjorths Hotel**, where they have a wonderful restaurant in the back. It eases the transition from beach bum back to civilised human being.

If you are into hiking and still have the energy, ask a member of the staff at the hotel to point out the way to Råbjerg Mile. You can follow the paved road or walk off the road, which is a little harder but much more interesting. After about 5km (3 miles) you

Gammel Skagen, threatened by sand dunes

might think that you have walked all the way to the east coast and that the water waits right behind the dunes. It is not so. You have reached **Råbjerg Mile**, a travelling sand dune that took off from the west coast hundreds of years ago, and is still moving slowly towards the east. In another 150 years, it will block the only road to and from Skagen and force future generations to come up with a creative response to nature's challenges.

From Råbjerg Mile, follow the road. A couple of potters have set up shop along the last stretch of the road, and their prices are somewhat lower than in the city. Catch the bus back, but don't go all the way to Skagen, get off in **Gammel Skagen** (Old Skagen) on the west coast. (Or you could jump on the bus in Kandestederne and let it take you all the way to Gammel Skagen. Don't stop at Råbjerg Mile, the next bus might be hours away).

Gammel Skagen lies where the fishermen first settled, hoping that they could make a living out of fishing in the North Sea. They could, but they had not foreseen that the land would be just as treacherous as the sea. As at Råbjerg Mile, the sand kept creeping up around their houses, and fighting the sand became as much of a concern as fighting the North Sea storms. The town we now know as Skagen grew up because life at the original Skagen had become simply too hard.

But if you arrive on a sunny summer's afternoon, Gammel Skagen looks inviting. It is not a big place – one paved main road and a dozen or two dirt roads. There are a couple of pleasant restaurants, but if you don't want to spend the money for dinner, try to get by on snack foods until sunset. One of the roads in Gammel Skagen is named **Solnedgangen** (The Sunset), and that is where you should be when everybody comes out to watch the sun dip into the sea.

Sunset, Gammel Skagen

Shopping

Denmark is known to be an expensive country, but that doesn't mean you can't find bargains. The tourist brochures will try to sell you fur coats and furniture and other such major investments, and they do a good job at that, so I'll concentrate on things that will fit in your suitcase and hopefully won't turn your wallet inside out.

A warm welcome for shoppers

Everything you purchase is subject to a 25 percent sales tax called MOMS. Non-EU residents can have this refunded on purchases of over 300kr from participating shops. Pick up a tax free brochure in one of the many shops that advertise tax free shopping.

Danish Design

Furniture, kitchenware, stereos, textiles, toys – anything that can be designed can also be labelled Danish design. The style is what counts. 'Form follows function' was the phrase that Scandinavian designers built their reputation on. The best place in Copenhagen to study the results is Illums Bolighus at Amagertorv 10 (with

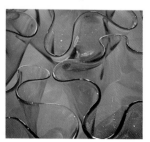

another branch at the airport) with a fine array of stylish furniture, glassware, lamps and tableware. The Bang & Olufsen shop at the far end of Stroget (3–5 Østergade) is the place for elegant stereo equipment. Department stores such as Illums and Magasin du Nord are also good places to look.

Danish glassware

Porcelain

Royal Copenhagen and Bing & Grøndahl are two famous labels in Danish porcelain. Today, they actually belong to the same company, but they still operate under both names. Visit the Copenhagen stores on Strøget (Amagertorv 6) or at the airport to study the many beautiful designs. But if you are not a collector and are just looking for a souvenir, buy a 'second' (slightly imperfect) or shop at one of the flea markets. You can recognise 'seconds' from the stamp on the bottom, which has been scratched a little by the factory – itself the best place to look *(see page 32)*.

Glass and ceramics

There has been something of a revival in glass over the past 15 years or so. In Copenhagen, traditional glassware can be purchased from Holmegaard at Østergade 15. Illums Bolighus has a large collection of new glasses, bowls and vases, which you can find in the capital and in gift stores around the country. There is a glass-blower in Skagen next to the train station, and he has colleagues in Copenhagen in Christiania and Rosenborg Garden (Kronprinsessegade 34B). In summer, glass-blowers demonstrate their art at the Glass Museum in Ebeltoft *(see page 51)*.

Similarly, there are a large number of potters at work these days. Their products are mainly sold in gift stores, but you can also buy directly from the craftsmen. Look out for "Keramik" signs along country roads.

Flea market browser

Flea markets

If you are visiting during the summer, don't miss the flea markets in Copenhagen. There is one on Israels Plads (close to Nørreport train station) and another in Smallegade at Frederiksberg behind the town hall. The dealers get most of their goods from estate sales, and you can always find blue-fluted Royal Copenhagen porcelain there, along with Christmas plates, crystal vases, Holmegaard glassware and other good stuff, if you take your time to weed through the junk to find the gems.

Silverware

In Copenhagen, Georg Jensen at Amagertorv 4 (as well as at the airport) offers an opulent array of jewellery, watches, cutlery and candle holders. Department stores such as Illum and Magasin du Nord also stock Danish-designed silverware.

Leather

If a fashion fur from Birger Christensen is not in your budget, how about a leather coat from one of the discount stores on Vesterbrogade in Copenhagen? You can get a good jacket for about 1,000kr (250kr deductable for MOMS).

Knitwear

When the cold, rainy-grey winter comes around, woollen sweaters are essential. That's why knitwear has become almost an art form in the Scandinavian countries. You'll find traditional patterns at Kaufmann (Nygade 2) and Sweater Market (Frederiksberggade 15), both on Strøget in Copenhagen. If you would like a more modern style, walk around the corner to Nicole Garn (Vestergade 12), where you can also buy the wool and patterns to the models on display.

Jewellery

Amber *(rav)* still washes up on the coast from time to time, and you'll find amber stores in all the tourist areas. You can get a pair of earrings for 75kr if you look around. Another Danish speciality is exact copies of Viking and Bronze Age jewellery (try Museums Kopi Smykker on Grønnegade and Frederiksberggade in Copenhagen, as well as at the airport; and at Kannikegade 12 in Århus).

Amber everywhere Halberstadt on Strøget in Copenhagen (Østergade 4) has its own tourist attraction: an 18-carat gold model train with wagons full of diamonds, rubies, emeralds and sapphires. In the side streets off Strøget, you can find jewellers who sell their own designs, for instance Guld & Gummi (Gammel Mønt 37) and Metal Point (Pilestræde 42). Erle Perle (Skindergade 33) doesn't care for silver and gold, but instead makes colourful earrings out of plastic, wood and other inexpensive materials.

Eiderdowns

Here's a secret that every Dane knows: to buy one of the fabulous Danish eiderdown comforters at half price, go to Jysk Sengetøjslager, a discount chain with outlets all around the country (in Copenhagen and Århus in several locations). Nobody can beat their prices. Remember to buy covers for your eiderdown, and ask the store to pack it tightly so you can travel with it (it won't do it any harm). Rather more on the tourist track is the Ofelia Down Comforter Centre, at 3 Amagertorv in Copenhagen; quality is excellent.

Food

Everything you've seen on the restaurant menus can also be found in the stores, but some things are easier to travel with than others, and not all foodstuffs can be taken into countries outside the EU. Although the speciality stores often have the highest quality, you will be better off if you shop in a supermarket, where the food is vacuum-packed. For instance, an ordinary, semi-strong Danish cheese has such a strong smell that it could ruin your suitcase if not properly wrapped. Guld Danbo or Klovborg are two of my favourites, not too strong but with a lot of taste. Then there is the black rye bread, the *leverpostej* (liver paté), the sweet-pickled cucumbers, the North Sea caviar, the smoked salmon, the biscuits and pastries, you name it... And don't miss the black salt liquorice. You'd have to be raised on the stuff to enjoy Piratos, but try Domino, Skiltelakrids and Saltbomber. If you prefer something sweet, Sømod (Nørregade 36 in Copenhagen) makes its own drops the old-fashioned way in all sizes and flavours.

Special Souvenirs

Toy theatres were popular in the old days. Hans Christian Andersen loved them, and you might too when you see the selection at Priors Dukketeatre in Copenhagen. They have the Royal Theatre in miniature, as well as whole plays in packages or in single figures. It's easy to get lost in this enchanting little world. Find them at Købmagergade 52; the store is closed at weekends.

And don't leave the country without a package of candles. Even if you bring nothing else home with you, you should buy this inexpensive little creator of genuine Danish *hygge*. For high-quality wooden toys try the Krea store on Vestergade in Copenhagen.

Pick and mix

Eating Out

Every neighbourhood has its own cafes. Take advantage of them. Most cafes have a quiche on the menu, as well as one or two salads, *chilli con carne*, different kinds of sandwiches and maybe a soup. You order and pay at the bar, and they'll bring the food to your table. It's simple, filling, inexpensive – and often delicious.

Danish beer, internationally famous

During a typical day, a Dane will eat bread with cheese or jam for breakfast, and maybe a portion of yoghurt or muesli. On Sundays, he'll go to the bakery and buy bread and pastries: *rundstykker, kryddere, tebirkes* and *chokoladeboller* (try them!). For lunch he'll have *smørrebrød* (open sandwiches) or a salad. In the afternoon, he might sneak out to the hot-dog stand, or buy pastries *(wienerbrød)* or a bag of candy to get him through the rest of the day. But what he'll eat for dinner is hard to predict. It might be a pizza, a load of potatoes with gravy and traditional meatballs *(frikadeller)*, a slice of lean meat with a salad on the side, or a spicy curry dish.

Traditional food often includes things that have been smoked, salted or pickled, while the younger generations prefer their dishes to be fresh, crisp and/or spicy hot.

Copenhagen

Traditional Danish Food

CAFÉ SORGENFRI
Brolæggerstræde 8
Tel: 33 11 58 80
If you can cut your way through the smoke, you're in for a treat: Danish smørrebrød served in an old-fashioned bar that hasn't changed for decades.

GRØFTEN
Tivoli
Tel: 33 12 11 25
VIPs and ordinary folk eat side by side in this old-fashioned Tivoli restaurant; speciality: shrimps on white bread.

Smørrebrød with cheese

CAFÉ EMMA
Østerbrogade 64
Tel: 35 26 09 52
A nice, old-fashioned cafe at Østerbro. The food is displayed behind glass, so you can point at what you want.

HACKENBUSCH
Vesterbrogade 124
33 21 74 74
Vesterbro's most popular cafe, a converted pharmacy, serves some of the best inexpensive meals in town.

KAFÉ RUST
Guldbergsgade 8
Tel: 31 35 00 33
You can't get good food any cheaper. It's luxury for budget travellers.

SOMMERSKO
Kronprinsensgade 6
Tel: 33 14 81 89
Sommersko has about 40 items on the menu, all of them good and very reasonably priced. The portions are huge. Always busy.

HANSENS GAMLE FAMILIEHAVE
Pile Allé 10–12
Tel: 36 30 92 57
Romantic courtyard. You are allowed to bring your own food, as long as you buy something to drink, but their food is inexpensive and good.

IDA DAVIDSEN
St Kongensgade
Tel: 33 91 36 55
Around the corner from Amalienborg Castle, this lunchtime institution is known to have had the Queen herself pop in for *smørrebrød* and aquavit. Reservations highly recommended; open for lunch only; closed at weekends.

NYHAVNS FÆRGEKRO
Nyhavn 5
Tel: 33 15 15 88
Specialises in seafood with an excellent herring buffet with bread and potatoes. Also has good *smørrebrød*.

Cafes

Although most cafes offer something to eat, the following have a larger selection of good food at affordable prices. They don't take reservations, just walk on in.

CAFÉ BARCELONA
Fælledvej 21
Tel: 31 35 76 11
Cafe downstairs and restaurant upstairs. The menu changes, but it's always good. Reservations are highly recommended.

A tradition of good service

Steak Houses

BASE CAMP
Holmen, Christianshavn
Tel: 70 23 23 18
A hot spot with live music, good food and an outdoor beach where you can grill your own steaks and seafood.

BRYGGERIET APOLLO
Vesterbrogade 3
Tel: 33 12 33 13
Brews its own beer and orders its own meat, but still keeps prices at a moderate level.

JENSENS BØFHUS
Kultorvet 15
Tel: 33 15 09 84
Also at: Gråbrødre Torv
Tel: 33 32 78 00
If you have a craving for steak, but cringe when you look at most establishments' prices, this place will save you and your wallet.

PEDER OXE
Gråbrødre Torv 11
Tel: 33 11 00 77
Serve yourself from the delicious salad bar while you wait for your steak.

Vegetarian

GOVINDAS
Nørre Farimagsgade 82
A popular Hare Krishna kitchen with an excellent buffet.

RIZ RAZ
Kompagnistræde 20
Tel: 33 15 05 75
Serve yourself from a large buffet of salads and vegetable dishes prepared Mediterranean-style. If the carnivore in you takes over, you can order meat on the side.

SHEZAN
Viktoriagade 22
Tel: 31 24 78 88
Half of Copenhagen knows and loves this family-run Indian restaurant on Vesterbro. The atmosphere is not exactly romantic – neon lights on the ceiling – but good cheap meals and generous helpings. Meat dishes are also available.

SPISE LOPPEN
Christiania
Slightly pricey, but mouthwatering food. Located in the heart of the famous Free State.

Delicious summer spread

Top of the Range

KOMMANDANTEN
Ny Aelgade
Tel: 33 12 09 90
Classical French/Danish cuisine. Two stars in the Michelin guide.

KONG HANS KÆLDER
Vingårdsstræde 6
Tel: 33 11 68 68
Located in the old wine cellars of King Hans (1455–1513). One star in the Michelin guide.

RESTAURATIONEN
Møntergade 19 at Vognmagergade
Tel: 33 14 94 95
The porcelain and candleholders are old but combined in an attractive postmodern way. The chef is young and inspired and the wine selection is excellent.

Something Sweet

LA GLACE
Skoubogade 3 (off Strøget)
Tel: 33 14 46 46
It would be a crime to leave without experiencing Denmark's famous treats. This is one traditional tea room you could try: sink your teeth into a big, sinful piece of sports-layercake or delicious homemade ice cream.

Århus

CAFÉ SMAGELØS
Klostertorv 7
Tel: 86 13 51 33
Famous for their arty brunch, which is a modern spin on the traditional open sandwiches. Amazing homemade bread.

EMMERYS
Guldsmedgade at Klostergade
Tel: 86 13 04 00
Spanish and Italian dishes. Open for breakfast, lunch and dinner.

...there's service with a smile

ESDRAGON
Klostergade 6
Tel: 86 12 40 66
The French chef serves some of the best food in town at moderate prices. Reservations recommended.

In every street...

JACOB'S BAR BQ
Vestergade 3
Tel: 86 12 20 42
Popular and lively place, open from 11am to midnight daily. Steaks, kebabs and seafood dishes. Located in an old merchants' house.

LE CANARD
Frederiksgade 74
Tel: 86 12 58 38
Classical, top-class French cuisine served in suitably elegant surroundings. Reservations recommended.

Smoked herring

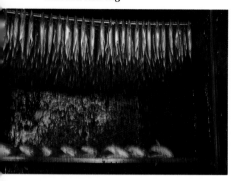

PIND'S CAFÉ
Skolegade 29
Tel: 86 12 20 60
An Århus institution. To see what all the fuss is about, order anything here with a shot of aquavit and a beer.

SKOVMØLLEN
At Moesgaard Museum
Tel: 86 27 12 14
A peaceful idyll in the woods 9km/6 miles south of Århus (bus 6). Wonderful for afternoon tea. Closed Monday.

TEATER BODEGA
Skolegade 7
Tel: 86 12 19 17
Traditional Danish food in a fun bar behind the theatre.

Danes prefer healthy food

Don't forget the cafes behind the cathedral. They serve excellent food at prices that are hard to beat.

Skagen

In Skagen, most hotels have their own excellent restaurants, eg Clausens Hotel and Brøndums Hotel. You should also check the Nightlife chapter *(opposite)* for addresses of cafes with dining menus.

Other recommendations include:

BODILLES KRO
Østre Strandvej 11
Tel: 98 44 33 00
Excellent Danish seafood dishes in a great atmosphere; near the harbour.

DE 2 HAVE
Grenen
Tel: 98 44 24 35
The northernmost restaurant in Denmark, with a view of the two oceans meeting; cafeteria upstairs.

JECKELS
Jeckelsvej 5
Tel: 98 44 63 00
A legendary, and expensive, restaurant in Gammel Skagen. Reservations are highly recommended.

RESTAURANT PAKHUSET
On the harbour
Tel: 98 44 20 00
A very popular cafe/restaurant situated in a restored fish warehouse on the marina. Live music every night in the summer and weekends in the winter.

Nightlife

Nights at Tivoli Gardens

For up-to-date information about events in Copenhagen, pick up the English-language *Copenhagen Post* and *Copenhagen This Week*. The Friday papers publish listings for the week to come. Ask at the tourist information office or at Use-It (Youth Information Centre) if you can't decipher it.

Copenhagen

Cafes

Most cafes are open till 1 or 2am, but a few stay open till 5am.

DAN TURELL
Store Regnegade 3–5
Thursday–Saturday till 5am.
Opened in 1978 and now rather run down, but a beloved second home to many art students.

EUROPA
Amagertorv 1
Nicest cafe on Strøget; international newspapers. Outdoor tables in summer.

KRASNAPOLSKY
Vestergade 10
Large and empty in the morning, crowded and 'hopping' at night.

NORDEN
Østergade 61
Art Nouveau-style cafe. Always a busy spot.

PARK CAFÉ
Østerbrogade 79
Noisy, but always swinging till late.

PUSSY GALORE'S FLYING CIRCUS
Skt. Hans Torv
Popular meeting place with a unique atmosphere.

SABINE'S CAFETERIA
Teglgårdsstræde 4
As local as it gets in the city centre.

SOMMERSKO
Kronprinsensgade 6
Opened in 1977 as the first French-style cafe, and still one of the liveliest.

Dining to music

VICTOR
Ny Østergade 8
Upscale restaurant and cafe, with elegance to match the prices.

Bars

ALLEENBERG
Allégade 4
Late-night bar for people who like to drink, smoke and talk.

FREUD'S
Gothersgade 19

Weird drinks and normal people mix well in this bar.

KGB
Dronningens Tværgade
Not the headquarters of the Russian Secret Police, but a great vodka bar nonetheless.

MUSEN & ELEFANTEN
Vestergade 21
The Danish equivalent of an English country pub.

OXE'S VINBAR
Gråbrødre Torv 11
Wine bar frequented by the young and rich-to-be.

PALÆ 4271
Ny Adelgade 5
Just about the best alternative to the cafes.

STEREO BAR
Linnésgade 16a
Trendy design bar with DJs and underground music. Seventies retro decor complete with lava lamps. Favourite pre-clubbing hangout.

With Live Music

MOJO BLUES BAR
Løngangsstræda 21
The perfect atmosphere to hear great blues music and drink good beer.

PUMPEHUSET
Studiestræde 52
Along with Loppen in Christiania, a club that books small to mid-sized rock, pop, indie and jazz acts.

RUST
Guldbergsgade 8
Live bands plus DJs. Also serves the cheapest meals in town. Has an outdoor yard and bar.

All the latest trends are here

VEGA
Enghavevej 40
Top venue featuring big names from the rock and dance scene as well as lesser-known acts.

Jazz Bars

COPENHAGEN JAZZ HOUSE
Niels Hemmingsensgade 10
Modern jazz with lots of ambience. Club night on weekends is popular with the younger jazz crowd.

FINN ZIEGLERS HJØRNE
Vodroffsvej 24
Neighbourhood bar and restaurant owned by a jazz violinist.

Discotheques

The music scene in Copenhagen is so lively that there are few pure discos. Admission charges start at 50kr. Dress up.

CLUB CLIMAX/MANTRA
Bernstorffsgade 3
Featuring techno, house and drum 'n' bass, and a luxurious interior. One of the city's coolest clubs.

ELECTRIC CIRCUS
Bernstorffsgade 3
Electronic dance music and morning-after clubbing.

HOUSE OF DANSE
Axeltorv 2
Wednesday and Thursday 10pm–3am; Friday and Saturday 11pm–5am. Fast-paced, modern disco with radio DJs.

LE KITSCH
Gothersgade 11
Hard-core dance club.

SABOR LATINO
Vester Voldgade 85

Salsa, usually with live bands, and a chance to take dance lessons.

Classical Music

RADIOHUSETS KONCERTSAL
Julius Thomsensgade 1
Tel: 31 10 16 22
(reservations taken by BilletNet in any post office)
Concerts with the Radio Symphony Orchestra and guests.

Ask about concerts in churches at the tourist information office (see page 79).

Theatres

The majority of theatres in Copenhagen are closed during the summer. You'll get the best information on what's going on from the tourist information office.

DET KONGELIGE TEATER (ROYAL THEATRE)
Kongens Nytorv
Tel: 83 14 10 02
Theatre, opera and ballet performances, September–May. Ask your travel agency for a performance schedule.

KANONHALLEN
Serridslevvej 2 (near Park Café)
Tel: 35 43 20 21
Open most of the year. International dance and theatre festivals during the summer.

THE LONDON TOAST THEATRE
Kochsvej 18
Tel: 33 22 86 86
The only English-language theatre in Copenhagen, showing plays of a high standard.

Cinemas

Films are shown in the original language with Danish subtitles. Look for newspaper listings. Some locations have cheaper seats on Monday.

CINEMA X
Kalvebod Brygge 57
Tel: 70 10 12 02
Multiplex with Scandinavia's largest screens.

GRAND
Mikkel Bryggersgade 8
Tel: 33 15 16 11
Art films and foreign films.

IMPERIAL
At Vesterport Station
Tel: 33 11 82 32
Large-screen cinema.

PALACE
Axel Torv 9
Tel: 33 13 14 00
Several screens in the same building.

PARK BIO
Østerbrogade 79
Tel: 31 38 33 62
Re-runs at low prices.

Breakfast Places

O'S AMERICAN BREAKFAST AND BARBEQUE
Gothersgade 15

Danish guests usually enquire about the 'hash browns' in this fun American-type cafe with good food and bad service.

SOMMERSKO
Kronprinsensgade 6
One of the best brunches in town; they open at 9am (10am Sunday).

Århus

Pick up a copy of *What's On in Århus* with listings of live music, art shows, theatre, cinema and more.

Live Music

BENT J.
Nørre Allé 66
Famous jazz bar; small with cosy ambience. Performances usually start at 9pm.

FATTER ESKIL
Skolegade 25
Excellent blues club.

GLAZZHUSET
Åboulevarden 35
(underneath the pedestrian street)
Large and airy jazz club.

TRAIN
Toldbodegade 6
Tel: 86 13 47 22.
Lots of top-class international talent plays live here. This is *the* place for late night disco.

VOX HALL
Vesterallé 15
Tel: 86 12 26 77.
Indie rock, folk and world music.

Discotheques

CAFÉ PARADIS
Paradisgade 7–9
Wednesday–Saturday 11pm–5am. Not a mainstream disco – just take

CINECITY
Skt. Kunds Torv 25
Tel: 70 13 12 11
One of the large, multi-screen cinemas in Århus, showing many movies in English, very near the central train station.

Skagen

In Skagen, most of the hotels have their own restaurants and bars. Some have live entertainment too, so check them out as you walk by.

BUDDY HOLLY
Havnevej 16
Restaurant and cafe with rock'n'roll music every night during the summer, followed by disco till 3am.

a look at the building. Free on Wednesdays and Thursdays.

EDISON
Frederiksgade 76
Free admission Friday and Saturday. Open 11pm–6am.

XS TECHNOCLUB
Klostergade 34
Techno, house, R&B and soul. Very popular with the young crowd.

FREGATTEN
Trondsvej 20
Sussi and Leo, infamous for their bad taste, play some favourites Tuesday–Saturday.

JAKOB'S CAFÉ AND BAR
Havnevej 4
A popular cafe and restaurant by day, fun bar by night. With live music and outdoor tables on the balcony. Great atmosphere.

Classical Music

MUSIKHUSET ÅRHUS
Thomas Jensens Allé
Tel: 86 13 343 44
All kinds of music, dance and theatre. Classical orchestras, opera and major artists.

Ask for a schedule of church concerts at the tourist information office.

SKAW PUBBEN
Havnevej 3
A tiny pub where you can also get traditional Skagen food.

STORM P/LA BAR
Havneplads 4
This bar is popular with all age groups.

Cinema

In Århus, cinema tickets are discounted on Wednesday.

ØST FOR PARADIS
Paradisgade 7–9
Tel: 86 19 31 22
Charming art cinema theatre.

VISEVÆRTSHUSET
Skt. Laurentii Vej 41
Pub with live music every night in summer, and at weekends in off-season.

Calendar of Special Events

JANUARY/APRIL

There is a reason why these months are not part of the tourist season. The weather is cold, the days are short, and the Danes themselves tend to hide in their homes, where they practise *hygge*, or being cosy. But when the trees start to sprout new leaves and Tivoli opens in late April, things begin to stir.

MAY

The Copenhagen Carnival, usually at the end of the month, features processions and concerts (rock, blues, jazz and folk). Get a full programme of events from the Tourist Office. On a Sunday in late May the Copenhagen marathon takes place.

JUNE

In mid-June, young conductors of classical music compete in the prestigious Malko contest in Copenhagen (Radiohuset).

By the end of the month, Roskilde calls. The rock festival in Roskilde is one of the oldest and largest of the many summer festivals, and it is always a success – even when it rains, as it often does.

Around the same time, there's a festival in Skagen, concentrating on ballads and folk music.

JULY

In early July, the Copenhagen Jazz Festival turns the city upside down with free concerts in the streets and more music in the clubs at night. And when the jazz musicians say good-bye to Copenhagen, some of them head to Århus to meet with other colleagues during the Århus International Jazz Festival in mid-July.

Free (or nearly free) rock concerts sponsored by the breweries have become a summer tradition in Denmark. Watch for posters headed *Grøn koncert* and concerts at *Femøren*.

A long, long time ago, people gathered to trade with the Vikings when they came home from their summer expeditions. Moesgaard Museum has revived this tradition south of Århus, and during the last weekend of July you can buy copies of the old produce and eat, drink and have fun with the Vikings.

AUGUST

The Danish National Opera has Strauss on the programme as an introduction to the Århus Festival Week. Call 89 31 82 70 if you'd like to know more about these marathon performances.

On the last weekend of August, the folk-oriented Tønder Festival, one of Europe's largest, gets underway. As well as folk acts, jazz and soul music are also represented. Tønder is located in South Jutland, just a few miles from the German border.

SEPTEMBER

From the first Saturday in September, Århus holds a giant cultural festival lasting for 8 or 9 days. Theatre groups, performance artists, and musicians of all kinds flock to the city, and you'd better reserve your hotel room as early as possible if you'd like to go to the party. Call 89 31 82 70 for more information.

OCTOBER

School children have the third week of October off. If you happen to be in Denmark during that week, there will be lots of things to do, but you'll have to share the buses, museums, etc. with lots of kids.

NOVEMBER

As the month separating the autumn holiday season from Christmas, November seems to have no separate identity. The wind is not as strong as in October, the mornings not quite as dark as in December. To make things worse, November is just as boring as it is grey.

DECEMBER

Christmas is celebrated on the night of the 24th, but the whole month is filled with Danish *hygge*. The *gløgg* (mulled wine), the fir festoons in the streets, the cakes, the darkness, the candles, the secrets and the sense of expectation give December a charm of its own.

Toy theatre celebrates Xmas

Practical Information

GETTING THERE

Copenhagen: From Kastrup Airport take the train or local bus 250S to the city centre. A taxi from the airport to the city costs around 150 kr. Trains run every 20 minutes and cost around 20kr. If you arrive in Denmark by rail, you might have to get off in Tåstrup. If so, jump on the first train to Københavns Hovedbanegård (the central railway station). Your ticket will be valid for this trip as well.

Århus: The cheapest way to get from Copenhagen (Valby Station) to Århus is by coach. Call 86 78 48 88 for more information. Trains from Copenhagen via Odense run hourly until 8pm. Call 70 13 14 15 to book. It's much quicker now that the Great Belt Bridge has been completed. An alternative is to take the plane to Tirstrup Airport, 45km (28 miles) to the northeast. Call 70 10 30 00. Buses run between the airport and the central train station in Århus.

Skagen: To get to Skagen by train or bus you have to change in Frederikshavn. The nearest airport is in Aalborg, 100km (62 miles) south.

GETTING ACQUAINTED

Denmark consists of 406 islands plus the large peninsula of Jutland. It all adds up to about 43,000 sq km (16,600 sq miles) with a coastline of 7,300km (4,500 miles). Some 5.3 million people live in the country, ruled by a prime minister and a queen who has only nominal power. Denmark is officially a Lutheran country with a state church. The social security system is one of the best in the world, and the taxes are among the highest.

The Great Belt Bridge

You'll feel welcome in this orderly little kingdom, where people are usually friendly and eager to help. Just observe three basic rules: do not litter, do not ignore red lights at crossings, and stay happy when you drink.

When to Visit

The high season is June, July and August. As with most of northern Europe, the weather is sometimes beautiful all summer, and sometimes cold and rainy from the end of June until the beginning of August. Weatherwise, I usually recommend mid-May through mid-June and August as the best times to visit. Then of course, there's Christmas, the peak time for Danish *hygge*. If you visit out of season, some attractions (like Tivoli) will be closed; on the plus side, you'll have the sites and museums almost to yourself.

Visas and Passports

If you are a citizen of Sweden, Norway, Iceland or Finland and arriving from one of those countries, you don't need a passport. If you are a citizen of Switzerland, Austria or an EU country, you can enter Denmark with certain other identity cards, but you'll have to check with your consulate.

With a few exceptions, everyone else needs at least a passport to enter the country. Citizens of the US, Canada, Australia, New Zealand, Japan, and most other countries do not need visas, but citizens of India, Pakistan or Turkey do. Check with your local Danish consulate before you leave home.

Customs

Denmark has stricter customs regulations than most EU countries. Those regarding liquor and cigarettes are frequently debated and are subject to change. To be safe, don't bring more than one litre of liquor with you, two litres of wine and one carton of cigarettes.

What to Pack

The Danes often wear several layers of clothes: a jacket or sweater above a shirt above a T-shirt, so they can strip off one or more layers as the temperature permits. If you visit during the summer, chances are that you will need both shorts and a sweater. An umbrella might come in handy too. Be sure to include some good walking shoes.

Electricity and Time

The voltage is 220v, and you'll be one time zone east of Greenwich Mean

A view of Danes

Time (add one hour to GMT). From the end of March to the end of September clocks are moved forward one hour (GMT +2).

Money Matters

The Danish currency is the kroner (crowns), and comes in notes in denominations of 1,000, 500, 200, 100 and 50kr. Coins are 20, 10, 5, 2 and 1 kr and 25 and 50 øre (ears). There are 100 øre in 1kr.

Banks generally charge a minimum fee of US$7 for changing traveller's cheques, although some require a

US$3.50 fee per cheque; others charge no fee but take a percentage of the amount you exchange, sometimes disguised as a low exchange rate.

Outside banking hours you can change money in the central railway station in Copenhagen, 7am–10pm daily (9pm during the winter).

Visa and MasterCard are accepted in most stores, while American Express is less popular. Many restaurants also accept Diners Club cards. If you are in need of cash, look for the numerous cash dispensers that can be used with most major credit cards. Tips and service charges are, in principle, included in all prices. The hairdresser will laugh if you try to tip him, but the maids at the hotel and a waitres at a bar will appreciate that you noticed their good work. Most of the time, 5–20kr, or ten percent, will do.

Safety

You don't have to be overly concerned about your personal safety during your visit. Even at night, the cities are generally safe. But during the summer pickpockets flock to the tourist areas, especially to Copenhagen. Never leave your purse or jacket out of sight. Be alert if several people try to get your attention at the same time, and keep your money close to your body.

GETTING AROUND

Denmark has excellent public transport. You won't need a car to follow most of the itineraries in this book, and indeed a car can be troublesome to manoeuvre around in the city – although quiet country roads make for pleasant driving. The cities are full of one-way streets, and parking alone will set you back 20kr per hour in central Copenhagen. If you bring your own car, you should park it on a side street outside of the parking zones and take the bus or a taxi to the city. The **Copenhagen Card** *(see page 77)* will let you ride on all buses and trains in the capital for free. Århus has several kinds of cheap bus tickets for tourists that are also valid for some sightseeing trips.

Car Rental

Car rental is expensive in Denmark, although you can save money by booking through an international agency before you leave home. You must be at least 20 years of age, although some companies stipulate 25 as the minimum age.

Companies inlcude Avis, Hertz and Europcar/InterRent.

Danish speed limits are 110km/h (70m/h) on motorways, 80km/h (50m/h) on major roads and 50km/h (30m/h) in the city. Green card insurance is not required for vehicles from other EU countries.

If you are driving, buy a Marguerit (Daisy) map to guide you along all the prettiest country roads.

Waiting for the bus

Great Bridges

Linking the islands of Funen and Zealand, and making it possible to drive all the way from Jutland to Copenhagen, the Great Belt Bridge opened in June 1998.

The Øresund Bridge links the capital with Sweden; making it just a short train ride away – ideal for a day trip.

Cycling

A bicycle will serve you better than a car on most of the itineraries in this book. The quality of rented bikes varies; in Skagen they are in perfect condition and have gears, whereas in Copenhagen they are often below the standard of the bikes you see in the streets. You have to leave a cash deposit, the size of which depends on the condition of the bike. Try to get hold of a copy of the Danish Cycling Federation's map, which has a wealth of information.

In Copenhagen, bikes can be borrowed from special bike racks around the city – all that is required is a 20kr deposit. Return the bike to any of the racks to get your deposit back. In other places, local tourist offices often rent bikes.

Taxis

Taxis are plentiful (but expensive) and it is possible to flag them down in the street. All taxis are metered. The service charge is included in the price, although of course a tip is always appreciated.

Copenhagen Card

This offers unlimited travel on buses and trains in Copenhagen, as well as free admission to over 60 local sights and museums, and discounts to other sights. The card is available in 24-, 48- and 72-hour versions costing 175kr, 295kr and 395 kr and can be purchased at the tourist office across from the central train station, the airport, many hotels and main railway stations.

EMERGENCIES

In case of fire or accident dial 112. Emergency calls are free.

Medical Services

Check the agreements on medical coverage with the authorities in your home country, preferably before you leave. EU citizens should bring an E111 form with them, which entitles the holder to free medical treatment. If you have to go to the hospital due to sudden illness, treatment is largely free to tourists from all nations.

Copenhagen: Dial 33 93 63 00 to get a doctor on call, Monday–Friday 8am–4pm. At night, call 38 88 60 41 in Copenhagen city, and 32 84 00 01 from Christianshavn.

Århus: Call 86 20 10 22, 4pm–8am and weekends.

Skagen: Monday–Friday 8am–4pm, dial 98 44 13 96, other hours 98 43 36 22.

Pharmacies

Copenhagen: Steno Apotek, Vesterbrogade 6C across from the central train station, tel: 33 14 82 66; 24hrs, service charge after business hours.

Århus: Løve Apoteket, Store Torv 5, tel: 86 12 00 22, 24hrs with service charge.

Skagen: Sct. Laurentii Vej 44, tel: 98 44 17 58.

Dentists

Copenhagen: Tandlægevagten, Oslo Plads 14; Monday–Friday 8am–9.30pm, Saturday–Sunday and holidays 10am– noon, tel: 35 38 02 51.

Århus: Tel: 86 19 77 07 outside office hours and at weekends..

Skagen: Call 98 44 28 70 or ask at the tourist information office.

Missing Credit Cards

American Express, tel: 80 01 00 21
Diners, tel: 36 73 73 73
MasterCard, Visa, Eurocard, Access, JCB, tel: 44 89 25 00

Lost Property

Copenhagen: The lost property office lies in Vanløse at Slotsherrensvej 113 (next to Islev S-train station), tel: 38

Even the city has quiet places

74 52 61. Hours are Monday–Thursday 9am–5.30pm, Friday to 2pm, closed Saturday and Sunday. If you lose something on the bus, call 36 13 14 15, daily 7am–9.30pm. If you lose something on the train, call 33 14 17 01, same hours.

Århus: The police station is located at Ridderstræde 1, tel: 87 31 14 48.

Skagen: The police station is at Rolighedsvej, tel: 98 44 14 44.

COMMUNICATIONS AND MEDIA

Telephone

The country code for Denmark is 45. To call foreign countries direct, dial 00 + the country code + the area code + the number. To get the operator, dial 113; to get information 118.

You can charge calls to the US on an AT&T card if you dial 80010010 (do not dial 00-1 first), to a Sprint card on 80010877 and to other credit cards on 80010022. Key country codes are: Australia (61); France (33); Germany (49); Italy (39); Japan (81); the Netherlands (31); New Zealand (64); Norway (47); Spain (34); Sweden 46; United Kingdom (44); United States and Canada (1).

To call from a public phone booth, lift the receiver, place coins in the groove on the top and dial. Pre-paid cards can be bought at any kiosk. Emergency calls are free (dial 112).

Post Offices

Copenhagen: Købmagergade 33, Tel: 33 32 12 12. Monday–Friday 9am–6pm, Saturday 9am–1pm; The Central Railway Station, Monday–Friday 8am–10pm, Saturday 9am–4 pm, Sunday 10am–5pm.

Århus: outside the central train station, Tel: 89 35 80 00. Monday–Friday 9am– 5.30pm, Saturday 9am–noon.

Skagen: Christian X's Vej 8, Tel: 98 44 23 44. Monday–Friday 9.30am –5pm, Saturday 9.30am–noon.

Media

Pick up a copy of the English-language *Copenhagen Post* for news in Denmark. The main libraries in Copenhagen and Århus have reading rooms with a huge selection of newspapers from around the world.

USEFUL INFORMATION

For the Disabled

A free brochure is available from the Danish Tourist Board, with information on accommodation, transportation and sights with wheelchair access. The Danish Handicap Association (Hans Knudsens Plads 1a 1st floor, 2100 Copenhagen Ø, Tel: 39 29 35 55) can also help you.

For Gay Visitors

The gay and lesbian society, Forbundet af 1948, operates two discotheques and cafes called Pan Club: Knabrostræde 3 in Copenhagen, tel: 33 13 19 48, and Jægergårdsgade 42 in Århus, tel: 86 13 43 80.

Babysitting

Studenternes Babysitting has been in business for 40 years and still operates at modest rates. Call well in advance on 70 20 44 16, Monday–Wednesday and Friday 10am–3pm, Thursday noon–6pm.

USEFUL ADDRESSES

Tourist Offices

Copenhagen: Wonderful Copenhagen has its headquarters at Bernstorffsgade 1, outside Tivoli and across from the central train station. For information or hotel bookings, call 70 22 24 42. See their excellent website at www.woco.dk.

Use-It at Rådhusstræde 13, is for backpackers and younger travellers. Call 33 73 06 20 or check www.useit.dk.

Århus: The Town Hall, tel: 89 40 67 00, Fax: 86 12 95 90, www.aarhustourist.dk.

Skagen: Sct. Laurentii Vej 22, tel: 98 44 13 77, Fax: 98 45 02 94, www.skagen-tourist.dk.

Embassies and Consulates

Australia: Strandboulevarden 122
Tel: 39 29 20 77
Canada: Kristen Bernikowsgade 1
Tel: 33 48 32 00
France: Kongens Nytorv 4
Tel: 33 15 51 22

In a romantic city

Germany: Stockholmsgade 57
Tel: 35 26 16 22
United Kingdom: Kastelsvej 40
Tel: 35 44 52 00
USA: Dag Hammerskjölds Allé 24
Tel: 35 55 31 44

Bookshops

THE BRITISH BOOK SHOP
Badstuestræde 8, Copenhagen
Tel: 33 93 11 15
Books in English.

BOGHALLEN, POLITIKENS HUS
Rådhuspladsen 35, Copenhagen
Tel: 33 11 85 11
Large selection of books in English.

G.E.C. GAD
Vimmelskaftet 32, Copenhagen
Tel: 33 15 05 58
Chain of shops with outlets in several cities.

STEVE'S BOOKS AND RECORDS
Ved Stranden 10, Copenhagen
Tel: 33 11 94 60
Specialises in jazz literature and records.

KRISTIAN F. MØLLER
Store Torv 5, Århus
Tel: 86 13 06 99
The best book shop in Århus.

JORGENSENS BOGHANDEL
Sct. Laurentii Vej 37, Skagen
Tel: 98 44 32 68

Traditional style

HOURS AND HOLIDAYS

Business Hours

Normal business hours are Monday–Friday 9am–5.30pm and Saturday 9am–1 or 2pm, although many shops stay open on Friday until 7 or 8pm. Bakeries usually open at 6am and non-food shops at 10am. Some supermarkets stay open till 7pm.

On the first Saturday of the month, most shops stay open until 4 or 5pm, and during the summer every Saturday is considered a 'long' Saturday. In tourist areas, hours are more flexible.

Banks are open Monday–Friday 9.30am–4pm, but Unibank stays open until 5pm. On Thursday, banks and public offices stay open until 6pm.

Public Holidays

New Year's Day: 1 January;
Easter: Maundy Thursday, Good Friday, and Easter Sunday and Monday;
Common Prayer Day: fourth Friday after Easter;
Ascension Day: 40th Day after Easter – always a Thursday;
Whit Monday: seventh Monday after Easter;
Constitution Day: 5 June. Shops close at noon, banks are closed all day;
Christmas: 24–26 December;
New Years' Eve: 31 December.

WHERE TO STAY

Most hotels will put in an extra bed for about a quarter of the cost of a separate room. Some also have group and family specials. Ask for weekend discounts. In Copenhagen most hotels give discounts in July, and in Skagen prices are lower during the winter.

In the listings below, Very Expensive means above 1,500 kr per night for a double room with shower (breakfast included), Expensive 1,000–1,500kr, Moderate 700–1,000kr, Inexpensive below 700kr. You'll get more for your money outside Copenhagen.

Copenhagen

There's a walk-in booking service at the tourist office, **Wonderful Copenhagen**, at Bernstorffsgade 1. To make reservations in advance, call the hotel directly.

Most of the hotels are situated around the central railway station, but another, more luxurious group are clustered in the area around Kongens Nytorv.

ASCOT HOTEL
Studiestræde 61
Tel: 33 12 60 00, Fax: 33 14 60 40
The beautiful hall of the former Copenhagen Baths serves as the lobby. Recently refurbished. Moderate to Expensive

CAB'INN COPENHAGEN
Danasvej 32–34
Tel: 31 21 04 00, Fax: 31 21 74 09
If all you need is a nice, clean room the size of a ship cabin and a shower in the morning, try this new concept. With a cafe downstairs, the Cab'Inn attracts many young travellers. Renovated in 1998. Inexpensive.

CLARION HOTEL NEPTUN
Skt. Annæ Plads 18
Tel: 33 13 89 00, Fax: 33 14 12 50
Preferred by business travellers, male and female. Conference facilities and a good restaurant, close to Nyhavn. Expensive

IBIS COPENHAGEN CROWN HOTEL
Vesterbrogade 41
Tel: 31 21 21 66, Fax: 31 21 00 66
Centrally located on busy Vesterbrogade, but no traffic noise. Children are just as welcome as business travellers. Expensive

HOTEL D'ANGLETERRE
Kongens Nytorv 34
Tel: 33 12 00 95, Fax: 33 12 11 18
Often rated the best hotel in Copenhagen. You can expect first-class service, but will have to pay for it. Very Expensive

HOTEL FY AND BI
Valby Langgade 62, Valby
Tel: 36 45 44 00, Fax: 36 45 44 09
A charming old hotel and restaurant in the centre of the old part of Valby. Only 10 minutes by bus or train to the city centre. Quiet and exceedingly quaint. Moderate

HOTEL KONG FREDERIK
Vester Voldgade 25
Tel: 33 12 59 02, Fax: 33 93 59 01
First-class hotel close to the town hall, famous for its restaurant. Expensive–Very Expensive

IBSENS HOTEL
Vendersgade 23
Tel: 33 13 19 13, Fax: 33 13 19 16
Popular hotel in a pleasant quiet street, run by three women. Inexpensive–Moderate

SOPHIE AMALIE HOTEL
Sankt Annæ Plads 21
Tel: 33 13 34 00, Fax: 33 11 77 07
Pleasant hotel close to the Hotel Neptun. Moderate–Expensive

Århus

ERIKSENS HOTEL
Banegårdsgade 6–8
Tel: 86 13 62 96, Fax: 86 13 76 76
Pleasant and inexpensive hotel a short distance from the town's railway station.

HOTEL LA TOUR
Randersvej 139
Tel: 86 16 78 88, Fax: 86 16 79 95
Motel-like, but nice, hotel north of the city. Inexpensive, with special offers if you arrive after 8pm without a reservation.

HOTEL MARSELIS
Strandvejen 25
Tel: 86 14 44 11, Fax: 86 11 70 46
Every room has an ocean view. Two km/one mile south of the city. Inexpensive to Moderate

HOTEL RITZ
Banegaardspladsen 12
Tel: 86 13 44 44, Fax: 86 13 45 87
Comfortable and centrally located with good service. Inexpensive

PLAZA HOTEL
Banegaardspladsen 14
Tel: 86 12 41 22, Fax: 86 20 29 04
Nice, clean hotel with good service and lots of single rooms on offer. Inexpensive

ROYAL HOTEL
Store Torv 4
Tel: 86 12 00 11, Fax: 86 76 04 04
Luxury accommodation in the centre of town. In-house casino. Expensive to Very Expensive

SAS RADISON
Margrethepladsen 1
Tel: 86 12 86 65, Fax: 86 12 86 75
Modern and luxurious hotel complete with top-class restaurant, meeting facilities and major conference centre. Centrally located. Very Expensive.

Skagen

To be or to do: that's the question when you visit the tip of Jutland. If you would like to see things and go places, you should stay in Skagen. If, on the other hand, you prefer to spend your time on the beach or sipping long drinks in a nice cafe with an ocean view, then you should head for Højen (Gammel Skagen) or Kandesterne. Activities here tend to be limited to hiking, swimming, surfing, beachcombing and other sea-related activities.

BADEPENSION MARIENLUND
Fabriciusvej 8, Skagen
Tel: 98 44 13 20, Fax: 98 45 14 66
Just 12 rooms in a charming old house in Skagen Vesterby. No showers in the rooms. Inexpensive

BRØNDUMS HOTEL
Anchersvej 3, Skagen
Tel: 98 44 15 55, Fax: 98 45 15 20
A well-known and traditional hotel next to Skagen Museum. Moderate

CLAUSENS HOTEL
Sct. Laurentii Vej 35, Skagen
Tel: 98 45 01 66, Fax: 98 44 46 33
Centrally located with a nice restaurant. Moderate

HJORTHS HOTEL
Kandesterne 17
Tel: 98 48 79 00, Fax: 98 48 78 01
Romantic old hotel, 300m (330 yds) from the beach. Inexpensive

HOTEL PETIT
Holstsvej 4, Skagen
Tel: 98 44 11 99, Fax: 98 44 58 50
Just 300m (330 yds) from the beach, which is as close to it as you can get in Skagen. Moderate

HOTEL SKAGEN STRAND
Hulsig
Tel: 98 48 72 22, Fax: 98 48 71 15
Apartments south of Skagen, close to transport. Inexpensive–Moderate

KOKHOLMS HOTEL
Kandestederne
Tel: 98 48 79 00, Fax: 98 48 78 01
Next to Hjorths Hotel (with which it shares its telephone and fax numbers) and just as pleasant. No single rooms. Moderate

NIELS SKIVERENS GAARD
Skiveren
Tel: 98 93 22 22, Fax: 98 93 22 59

Located 27km (17 miles) south of Skagen, close to the beach and a golf course. Apartments for up to four persons. Moderate

Ruths Hotel
Hans Ruthsvej 1, Gammel Skagen
Tel: 98 44 11 24, Fax: 98 45 08 75
One of the few hotels in Gammel Skagen that hasn't been turned into timeshare apartments. Moderate to Expensive

Skagen Sømandshjem
Østre Strandvej 2, Skagen
Tel: 98 44 25 88, Fax: 98 44 30 28
Hotel for sailors, but others are welcome too. Inexpensive

Summerhouses and Apartments

DanCentre
Søtorvet 5, Copenhagen
Tel: 70 13 13 14, Fax: 70 13 70 74
Grenåvej 530, Århus
Tel: 86 34 21 22, Fax: 70 13 13 12
Rents summerhouses all around the country.

H.A.Y. 4U
Kronprinsensgade 10
Tel: 33 33 08 05, Fax: 33 32 08 04
Rents apartments in the Copenhagen area for a minimum of three days.

Bed and Breakfast

Bed and breakfast in Denmark often just means bed and kitchen access. Ask what you get. Rooms cost 100-250kr depending on the location, or about half of what the cheapest hotel room will set you back.

In Århus and Skagen, the tourist information office will find a room for you for a nominal fee.

Youth Hostels and Sleep-Ins

To stay at youth hostels you need a valid YHA membership card, obtainable in your home country before you leave, or in Denmark (125kr) from the Danish Youth Hostel Association, Vesterbrogade 39, Copenhagen; tel. 31 31 36 12, fax. 31 31 36 26.

The Royal Hostel
Kronprinsensgade 10, Copenhagen
Tel: 33 33 08 05, Fax: 33 32 08 04
This wonderful little hostel is located right in the centre of the city. Call to make reservations, then post a deposit.

Århus City Sleep-in
Havnegade 20, Århus
Tel: 86 19 20 55, Fax: 86 19 18 11
Everybody is welcome – YHA membership not necessary. Inexpensive, with many single rooms.

Skawhostel Gammel Skagen
Højensvej 32, Gammel Skagen
Tel: 98 44 13 56, Fax: 98 45 08 17

Camping

Unfortunately, you cannot camp outside an authorised campground – camping in the fields etc. is prohibited by law.

The international influence on Danish cuisine has made the menus easier to decode in recent years. But when it comes to traditional Danish dishes, you'll need assistance. These are the basics, but don't hesitate to ask the waiter.

Morgenmad	Breakfast
Frokost	Lunch
Middag	Dinner
Smørrebrød	Open face sandwiches
Rugbrød	Black (rye) bread
Franskbrød	White (wheat) bread
Flûte	Crusty white bread
Bolle	Roll
Sild	(Pickled) herring
Tartar	Steak tartar
Leverpostej	Liver paté
Ost	Cheese
Fisk and *Skaldyr*	Fish and Shellfish
Fiskefilet	Fillet of fish
Rødspætte	Plaice
Forel	Trout
Tun	Tuna
(Røget) laks	(Smoked) salmon
Stjerneskud	Fillet of fish with shrimp and asparagus
Rejer	Prawns
Fjordrejer	Freshwater shrimps
Muslinger	Mussels
Hummer	Lobster
Grøntsager	Vegetables
Kartofler	Potatoes
Løg	Onion
Champignon	Mushrooms
Bønner	Beans
Gulerod	Carrot
Majs	Corn
Kål	Cabbage
Salat	Lettuce/Salad
Tomat	Tomato
Agurk	Cucumber

Copenhagen: The campground closest to the city is situated in Bellahøj at Hvidkildevej, tel: 31 10 11 50, open May 31–August 31 (bus No 2 to town).

The nicest is Strandmøllen Camping 14km north of the city at Strandmøllevej 2 in Klampenborg, tel: 45 80 94 45, open May–mid-September (take the S-train to Klampenborg station and then bus No 388).

Absalon Camping in Rødovre at Korsdalsvej 132, tel: 31 41 06 00 is open all year round.

Århus: The nicest place to camp is Blommehaven 4km (2½ miles) south of the city (take bus 6 or 19). It is situated by the sea in Marselisborg woods and open mid-April–mid-September. To make reservations, call them on tel: 86 27 02 07, or fax: 86 27 45 22.

Skagen: There are several campgrounds around Skagen, all of them very popular. It's advisable to make reservations in advance with the tourist office. Grenen Camping just north of the city, Fyrvej 16, tel: 98 44 25 46 is a good site

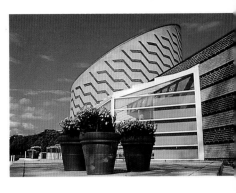

The Planetarium

Hovedretter	*Entrées*
Flæskesteg	Pork roast
Frikadeller	Meatballs
Mørbradbøf	Tenderloin (often cooked in a sauce)
Bøf	Steak
Hakkebøf	Burger
Kylling	Chicken
Kalkun	Turkey
Desserter	Desserts
Pandekager	Pancakes
Lagkage	Layercake
Småkage	Cookies
Kransekage	Marzipan stick
Wienerbrød	Pastry
Is	Ice cream, ice

ATTRACTIONS

Below is a selection of museums and sights that didn't fit into any of our itineraries, but we feel are worth a visit. Bus No 388 (from Lyngby Station to Helsingør Station) passes by Ordrupgaard, Rungstedlund and Nivågård.

Copenhagen

TYCHO BRAHE PLANETARIUM AND OMNIMAX THEATRE
Gammel Kongevej on Lake Sankt Jørgen
Tel: 33 12 12 24
Tuesday–Thursday 9.45am–9pm, Friday–Monday 10.30am–9pm
Large, modern planetarium with Omnimax theatre. Admission varies from 15–75kr depending on what you'd like to see.

THORVALDSENS MUSEUM
Porthusgade 2
Tel: 33 32 15 32
Tuesday–Sunday 10am–5pm
The works and collections of Danish sculptor Bertel Thorvaldsen (1770–1844) in a beautiful building next to Christiansborg. Admission: adults 20kr, children free.

DAVIDS SAMLING
Kronprinsessegade 30
Tel: 33 13 55 64
Tuesday–Sunday 1–4pm
Islamic art and European applied arts from the 18th century. Free admission.

ORDRUPGAARD
Vilvordevej 110, Charlottenlund
Tel: 39 64 11 83
Tuesday–Sunday 1–5pm
French impressionists and Danish 19th-century painters. Admission: adults 60kr, children free.

THE KAREN BLIXEN MUSEUM
Rungstedlund
Rungsted Strandvej 111
Tel: 45 57 10 57
May–September: daily 10am–5pm
October–April: Wednesday–Friday 1–4pm, Saturday–Sunday 11am–4pm
The home of Karen Blixen (Isak Dinesen), author of *Out of Africa*. Admission: adults 35kr, children free.

NIVÅGÅRD ART COLLECTION
Gammel Strandvej 2
Tel: 49 14 10 17
16th–19th century paintings from the Netherlands, Italy and Denmark. Adults 35kr, children free.

Århus

MOESGAARD MUSEUM OF PREHISTORY
Moesgaard Allé 20
Tel: 89 42 11 00
April–October: daily 10am–5pm; January–March and November–De-

cember: Tuesday–Sunday 10am–4pm
From the Stone Age to the Viking
era. In the woods near the beach (take
bus 6). Viking Meet, last weekend of
July. Adults 35kr, children free.

TIVOLI FRIHEDEN
Skovbrynet
Tel: 86 14 73 00
May–mid-June 1–10pm, mid-June–

August: 1–11pm
Amusement park south of the city.
Admission: adults 35kr, children 15kr.

THE WOMEN'S MUSEUM
Domkirkeplads 5 (behind the Cathedral)
Tel: 86 13 61 44
June–September: daily 10am–
5pm; other months: Tuesday–Sunday
10am–4pm
The modern history of women. Admission: adults 25kr, children free.

LEGOLAND
Billund in mid-west Jutland
Tel: 75 33 13 33

April–end October: 9am–9pm
The original of the famous park of
miniature landscapes built entirely
from Lego bricks. You can join a
Centrum Turist tour (Tel: 86 19 00
00) from Århus or purchase a special
Legoland ticket at the railway station. Admission: adults 150kr, children 140kr.

Skagen

EAGLE WORLD
Tuen, on the road to Hirtshals
Tel: 98 93 20 31
April–September
Eagles and falcons live safely in the
wild out here, but there are still
plenty of opportunities to get up
close and personal with them. Visitors are admitted to the park only
from 9–10am and 4–5pm.

LANGUAGE

Danish spelling is somewhat arbitrary. Most vowels have more than
one pronunciation (like the English
'i' in 'win' and 'wine'), and you can't
always tell from the spelling which
one to use. Just to make it all the
more confusing, Danish also makes
frequent use of a glottal stop, which
is not reflected in the spelling, plus
three or four more vowels than most
languages. And then there's the question of dialects. So don't expect to
become fluent in a month. Luckily,
most Danes speak English and will be
happy to volunteer their assistance
when you need it. You can get a long
way with German too. But if you'd
still like to try to make sense of street
signs and the like, these are the basic
rules for pronunciation:

a – a, as in 'cat' or as in French 'la'
e – as in 'bed' or, as an ending vowel,
     just like ø
i – ee as in 'sleep'

o – as in 'more' or just like å
u – u, as in 'put'
y – say 'ee', round your lips
æ – as in 'bear'
ø – as in 'fur' or say æ while you round your lips
å – aw, as in 'paw'

90	*halvfems*
100	*hundrede*
200	*tohundrede*
300	*trehundrede*
1000	*tusind*
2000	*totusind*

Days of the Week

Mandag (Monday), *tirsdag, onsdag, torsdag, fredag, lørdag, søndag.*

Months of the Year

Januar (January), *februar, marts, april, maj, juni, juli, august, september, oktober, november, december.*

The 24th of January 2001 is written: *24. januar 2001* or *1.24.2001*

Numbers

1	*en/et*
2	*to*
3	*tre*
4	*fire*
5	*fem*
6	*seks*
7	*syv*
8	*otte*
9	*ni*
10	*ti*
11	*elleve*
12	*tolv*
13	*tretten*
14	*fjorten*
15	*femten*
16	*seksten*
17	*sytten*
18	*atten*
19	*nitten*
20	*tyve*
21	*en-og-tyve*
22	*toogtyve*
23	*treogtyve*
30	*tredive*
40	*fyrre*
50	*halvtreds*
60	*tres*
70	*halvfjerds*
80	*firs*

Words and Phrases

goddag	hello
farvel	goodbye
hej	(replaces both the above)
godmorgen	good morning
godnat	good night
ja, jo	yes
nej	no
tak	thank you
ja tak	yes, please
nej tak	no, thanks
gade	road
vej	way
sti	trail
allé	avenue
plads or *torv*	square

gård	courtyard
have	garden
ingen adgang	no admittance
må ikke berøres	do not touch
tilladt	allowed
forbudt	forbidden
gratis	free
værelser	rooms
med bad	with shower
udsigt	view
etage or *sal*	floor

The ground floor is called *stuen*. First floor is the floor above *stuen*.

nord, nordre	north, northern
syd, søndre	south, southern
øst, østre	east, eastern
vest, vestre	west, western
gammel	old
ny	new

'Please' does not correspond to one word or phrase, but is expressed in the construction of the sentence. Danes will often forget to say 'please' in English, but don't mean to be rude.

SPORT

Copenhagen This Week has extensive listings of bowling and badminton halls, boat rental companies and much more. In Århus and Skagen, look for local posters. Ask local tourist infor-mation offices to assist you in finding and buying tickets for spectator sports.

Swimming

There is easy access to good white sand beaches just about anywhere in the country. A blue flag denotes that the beach is clean and the water clear. Swimming can occasionally be dangerous, especially on the west coast. Use common sense, and stay out of the water whenever the red flag is flying. On the west coast, climbing the dunes can be dangerous and is strictly prohibited.

Sailing, Canoeing and Waterskiing

JOHANNE LOUISE
Tel: 86 28 88 55
Organised trips on the sailing ship of the same name, moored at Marselis-borg Lystbådehavn marina. Special ar-rangements for parties. May–October.

KALØVIG BÅDEHAVN
Tel: 86 99 19 67, Fax: 86 99 45 38
Boat rental in Rønde north of Århus.

MOESGAARD STRAND KIOSK
Boat rental, take bus No 19 from Århus to Moesgaard Strand.

Skating

ÅRHUS SKØJTEHAL
Gøteborg Allé
Tel: 86 16 50 77
Ice rink, open September–March.

Fishing

There are good opportunities in vir-tually every area of the country, but you must obtain a local fishing li-cence (available from tourist offices) before you go out.

Horse Riding

MOESGAARD STRAND, ÅRHUS
Tel: 86 22 55 44
Weekdays 10am–2pm

Guided tours through the woods, June–August. Take bus 19.

VILHELMSBORG MANOR HOUSE
Bedervej 101, Mårslet at Århus
Tel: 86 93 71 11, Fax: 86 93 74 72
Manor house turned into an equestrian centre. For information, see www.vilhelmsborg.dk.

FURTHER READING

Background Reading

An Outline History of Denmark, by Helge Seidelin Jacobsen, Høst and Søn, 1990.
An Account of Denmark as it was in the year 1692, by Robert Molesworth, Wormanium, 1989.
A History of Denmark, by Palle Lauring, Høst, 1986.
Facts about Denmark, Ministry of Foreign Affairs, frequent updates.
Prehistoric Denmark, National Museum of Denmark, 1978.
Signposts to Denmark, by Anne Warburton (former British ambassador to Denmark), Hernov, 1992.

Historisk Atlas Danmark, edited by Jette Kjærulff Hellesen and Ole Tuxen. GEC Gads Forlag, 1988.

Guidebooks

Insight Guide: Denmark, Apa Publications, 2000.
Insight Compact Guide: Denmark, Apa Publications, 1998.
Insight Compact Guide: Copenhagen, Apa Publications, 2000.
Tivoli – The Magic Garden, by Ebbe Mørk, Høst and Søn, 1988.
On a Tour to Nordsjælland, by Ole Schierbeck, Høst and Søn, 1989.
Café – The Café Guide to Copenhagen, Per Kofoed, 1992.

Souvenir Books

Hans Christian Andersen's Denmark, Rhodos, 1983.
Copenhagen – Open Spaces and *Copenhagen – Interiors*, by Peder Olesen, Borgen, 1991.
Green Denmark, by Anders Tvevad, Skarv•Høst and Søn, 1992.
Denmark, by Sven Skovmand and Henrik Saxgren, Hedeskov, 1988.

Index

ART & Photo Credits

Photography by **Marianne Paul** *and*
5B, 6/7, 23, 58B **Jerry Dennis/APA**
Pages 18, 21T, 22T, 23, **Danish Tourist Board**
29T, 46T, 46B, 68, 71, 72, 74, 86

12 **Bert Wiklund**
16 **Press Association/Topham**
16, 73 **Topham Picturepoint**
Front cover **Greg Evans**
Back cover **Jeroen Snijders/APA**
Handwriting **V. Barl**
Cartography **Berndtson & Berndtson**
Cover design **Tanvir Virdee**

The travel guides that replace a tour guide - now better than ever with more listings and a fresh new design

INSIGHT
Pocket Guides

Insight Pocket Guides pioneered a new approach to guidebooks, introducing the concept of the authors as "local hosts" who would provide readers with personal recommendations, just as they would give honest advice to a friend who came to stay. They also included a full-size pull-out map. Now, to cope with the needs of the 21st century, new editions in this growing series are being given a new look to make them more practical to use, and restaurant and hotel listings have been greatly expanded.

INSIGHT GUIDES

The world's largest collection of visual travel guides

Now in association with

Also from Insight Guides...

Insight Guides is the classic series, providing the complete picture with expert and informative text and stunning photography. Each book is an ideal travel planner, a reliable on-the-spot companion – and a superb visual souvenir of a trip. 193 titles.

Insight Maps are designed to complement the guidebooks. They provide full mapping of major destinations, and their laminated finish gives them ease of use and durability. 100 titles.

Insight Compact Guides are handy reference books, modestly priced yet comprehensive. The text, pictures and maps are all cross-referenced, making them ideal books to consult while seeing the sights. 127 titles.

INSIGHT POCKET GUIDE TITLES

Aegean Islands
Algarve
Alsace
Amsterdam
Athens
Atlanta
Bahamas
Baja Peninsula
Bali
Bali Bird Walks
Bangkok
Barbados
Barcelona
Bavaria
Beijing
Berlin
Bermuda
Bhutan
Boston
Brisbane & the
 Gold Coast
British Columbia
Brittany
Brussels
Budapest
California,
 Northern

Canton
Cape Town
Chiang Mai
Chicago
Corfu
Corsica
Costa Blanca
Costa Brava
Costa del Sol
Costa Rica
Crete
Croatia
Denmark
Dubai
Fiji Islands
Florence
Florida
Florida Keys
French Riviera
 (Côte d'Azur)
Gran Canaria
Hawaii
Hong Kong
Hungary
Ibiza
Ireland
Ireland's Southwest

Israel
Istanbul
Jakarta
Jamaica
Kathmandu Bikes
 & Hikes
Kenya
Kraków
Kuala Lumpur
Lisbon
Loire Valley
London
Los Angeles
Macau
Madrid
Malacca
Maldives
Mallorca
Malta
Manila
Melbourne
Mexico City
Miami
Montreal
Morocco
Moscow
Munich

Nepal
New Delhi
New Orleans
New York City
New Zealand
Oslo and Bergen
Paris
Penang
Perth
Phuket
Prague
Provence
Puerto Rico
Quebec
Rhodes
Rome
Sabah
St. Petersburg
San Diego
San Francisco
Sarawak
Sardinia
Scotland
Seville, Cordoba &
 Granada
Seychelles
Sicily

Sikkim
Singapore
Southeast England
Southern Spain
Sri Lanka
Stockholm
Switzerland
Sydney
Tenerife
Thailand
Tibet
Toronto
Tunisia
Turkish Coast
Tuscany
Venice
Vienna
Vietnam
Yogjakarta
Yucatán Peninsula